HAUNTED ONTARIO 4

HAUNTED ONTARIO 4

ENCOUNTERS WITH GHOSTLY SHADOWS, APPARITIONS, AND SPIRITS

TERRY BOYLE

DUNDURN
TORONTO

Unless otherwise noted, all images belong to the author.

Editor: Cheryl Hawley
Design: Laura Boyle
Cover Design: Courtney Horner
Cover Image Credit: © Alexander Dunkel | istockphoto.com
Printer: Webcom

Library and Archives Canada Cataloguing in Publication

Boyle, Terry, author
       Haunted Ontario 4 : encounters with ghostly shadows, apparitions, and spirits / Terry Boyle.

Issued in print and electronic formats.
SBN 978-1-4597-3119-6 (pbk.).--ISBN 978-1-4597-3120-2 (pdf).-- ISBN 978-1-4597-3121-9 (epub)

1. Ghosts--Ontario. 2. Apparitions--Ontario. I. Title. II. Title: Haunted Ontario four.

BF1472.C3B687 2015   133.109713   C2015-900589-2
                                           C2015-900590-6

1 2 3 4 5   19 18 17 16 15

We acknowledge the support of the **Canada Council for the Arts** and the **Ontario Arts Council** for our publishing program. We also acknowledge the financial support of the **Government of Canada** through the **Canada Book Fund** and **Livres Canada Books**, and the **Government of Ontario** through the **Ontario Book Publishing Tax Credit** and the **Ontario Media Development Corporation.**

Care has been taken to trace the ownership of copyright material used in this book. The author and the publisher welcome any information enabling them to rectify any references or credits in subsequent editions.
— *J. Kirk Howard, President*

The publisher is not responsible for websites or their content unless they are owned by the publisher.

Printed and bound in Canada.

VISIT US AT
Dundurn.com | @dundurnpress | Facebook.com/dundurnpress | Pinterest.com/dundurnpress

Dundurn
3 Church Street, Suite 500
Toronto, Ontario, Canada
M5E 1M2

For my friends Nick and Robin Poulakis, who share their love of the paranormal with me, and my wife, Allanah O'Boyle, for her editing assistance

Contents

Introduction

Haunted Ontario 4 is a compilation of *Haunted Ontario 2, Marilyn at French River*, and new stories.

I first penned *Haunted Ontario* fifteen years ago. In that time I have completed four books on the subject of spirits, and hosted the popular national television show *Creepy Canada*. I have interviewed so many people who have seen, felt, or heard a spirit presence. One only has to listen to them and look into their eyes to know just how real their personal experience was to them. After all, how does anyone explain a push from behind by an unseen force, a bed that levitates three feet off the floor, a shadow that skirts by the corner of your eye, a full apparition that is visible for only a moment before it's gone? How does an object float through the air on its own and then drop to the floor at your feet? (That was my own experience as written up *Haunted Ontario.*) We can only theorize.

For sixteen years I have conducted historical and haunted walking tours in Parry Sound and Muskoka. During the tours I have seen pictures taken of people, who were neither on the tours nor anywhere near them, standing beside houses or jails or in group shots.

People have reported being touched by something or overcome with a chill, even though it is a warm summer evening. Other people have photographed unusual energy patterns floating in the air, inside or outside buildings and above tree tops. These are their experiences.

I have endeavoured to introduce my readers to places that are open to the public, such as museums, theatres, opera houses, former jails, and inns or hotels. I want you to be able to visit these places and investigate and experience things for yourselves.

You can never prepare to experience the unexplained. The reason is simple: you never know when something is going to happen, and when it does it is always startling and unnerving at first. The rational mind struggles to accept what it cannot explain.

Imagine for a moment that you are a person having lunch in a restaurant. You excuse yourself from the table to visit the washroom. While standing in front of the mirror, you see your image disappear and another face looks back at you! What would you do in that moment? How would you feel? Shocked? Panicked? Disbelieving?

There are many stories about spirits appearing in mirrors. A woman appears in the ladies' room mirror at the Jester's Court Restaurant in Port Perry; a spirit appears in the mirror of the ladies' washroom in the Bala Bay Hotel in Bala; the mirror in the officers' quarters of Fort George in Niagara-on-the-Lake sometimes contains the image of a woman. Many paranormal experts believe that mirrors act as portals or openings for spirits to move through. If we study the past we find examples of this belief. Not that long ago our ancestors would cover the mirrors in the house or turn them to the wall for three days when a death occurred in the family. The belief was that the deceased could find a way back through the mirror.

Anne Ridge, in her book *Death Customs in Rural Ireland*, states,

> Prayers were said, candles were kept burning, and holy water was sprinkled around the deathbed, to guard against evil. It was a common custom to cover all polished surfaces or mirrors, or to turn them to the wall.
>
> This has variously been explained as a means of preventing the spirit of the dead person from seeing its own

reflection and refusing to leave or as a means of preventing the spirit from taking the reflection or double of another person already caught there.

Another international custom was to open doors and windows to give the spirit free passage. Clocks were sometimes stopped. In some parts of England every bolt and lock in the house was unfastened when someone died.

Anne Ridge also writes,

> Candles were lit "to protect the body from evil spirits and other dangers as well as to illuminate the deceased's journey to the other world." Blessed candles were used at the time of death and afterward ordinary candles were used according to information gathered in the midlands. It has been recorded that an uneven number were used; three to five was the general rule. The candles were lit immediately the corpse was "left out" and were kept burning for the course of the entire wake.
>
> The butts of the candles had cures associated with them, particularly the first candles to have been lit.

According to Anne, from another source, if a person had a bad chest cold or bronchitis, the butts of the candles should be melted onto brown paper, which should be put on the chest.

In my book *Full Moons and Black Cats* I state, "If a candle, that was lit as part of a ceremony, went out, it was a sign that evil spirits were nearby."

Beliefs about the spirit world are sprinkled throughout our folklore, our beliefs, and our superstitions. For centuries we have acknowledged the existence of spirits. Our ancestors went to great measures to protect themselves and their dead. Many people still practise these ancient beliefs.

Haunted Ontario 4 is another venture into the spirit world. I trust the stories will captivate your imagination. Light a candle, turn the page, and enjoy!

Terry Boyle
November 2014

Blinkbonnie Inn

~ Gananoque ~

He loved his home. It was history, his family, his power, and his prestige. He could not let it go — not for anything. Not even death.

Everyone experiences some form of attachment. This yearning for association to a place, a person, or possessions can begin in youth and sometimes live even beyond the grave.

Charles MacDonald suffered from a yearning attachment. In his case it was to Blinkbonnie, his ancestral home. He was, after all, the last MacDonald to bear witness to an incredible journey dating back to 1810 in Gananoque, Ontario.

Gananoque is known as the Canadian gateway to the Thousand Islands. The name is a First Nations word that means both "land which slopes toward the water and disappears under it", and "place of good health".

One of the first land claims in the area was by Loyalist Joel Stone, who travelled to England in 1783 to petition for compensation for his losses in the American Revolution. Stone arrived in the area in 1787. There were two falls on the Gananoque River and for that reason he requested a land grant on both sides of the river. (Stone spelled the name of the place Cadanoryhqua and then Ganenoquay. In all, there have been fifty-two variations of the spelling of Gananoque. The present-day spelling first appeared in the 1820s.)

At the same time, Sir John Johnson, leader of a congregation of Loyalists from the Mohawk Valley and a member of the Executive Council, also petitioned for the same land. Johnson was granted one thousand acres on the east side of the Gananoque River and Stone was granted seven hundred acres on the west side. The first store, grist mill, and tavern were opened in 1792 by Stone.

The next stage of growth did not occur until Charles McDonald arrived in 1810 from New York State. He soon became a business partner with Stone and only one year later he married Stone's only daughter, Mary.

In 1812, Charles built a new frame home for his wife. He named his house Blinkbonnie, a Scottish name meaning "good to the eyes" or "good view." Charles persuaded his brother John, of New York State, to join him in partnership on January 17, 1818, under the firm name C. & J. McDonald. By 1824 the brothers had acquired the property that had originally been granted to Sir John Johnson, on the east side of the river. Now that had the river to generate power. A survey established the site for the village of Gananoque.

Two years later the McDonalds build the largest flour mill in Canada. At one time it was estimated that one quarter of all the flour sent to Montreal came from the Gananoque mill.

Unfortunately, Charles McDonald died in 1826, at the age of forty. A fire destroyed Blinkbonnie that same year. Charles' eldest son, William Stone MacDonald (he changed the spelling of his surname), joined his late father's firm in 1833. Blinkbonnie was completely restored and expanded by 1843. William lived at Blinkbonnie with his wife, Isabella Hall, and cared for his invalid mother during the restoration years.

William and Isabella's son, Charles, was born in 1837, and became a civil engineer. In 1869 he opened an office in New York City, where he was appointed a trustee in the building of the Brooklyn Bridge. When William Stone MacDonald died in 1902, Charles inherited the property. He made extensive renovations to the main house and the surrounding buildings.

When Charles's wife died in 1912, he gave his son, William, all the property and securities of the MacDonald family.

William, known about town as Mr. Willie, lived in Brooklyn, New York, but spent his summers at Blinkbonnie with his father, Charles. William died of a sudden heart attack in 1920 without a will and all the holdings, including Blinkbonnie, were sold to settle the estate. Charles wept at the prospect of losing the ancestral home.

~ ~ ~

School teacher Rebecca Edwards purchased Blinkbonnie in 1923, and proceeded to convert the property into a summer hotel. Charles MacDonald begged Miss Edwards to allow him to take up residence at his beloved Blinkbonnie for his remaining years. Fortunately she was delighted to let him do so. She even searched for some of the family antiques that had been sold to furnish his living quarters. Those she could not find she replaced with objects of equal age and style. Charles, restored to his original home, was a fortunate and happy man. He died in 1928, but many feel he never did leave Blinkbonnie.

Blinkbonnie's reputation as one of the finest hotels in the Thousand Islands spread far and wide. This fame was deserved, for the accommodations were excellent and the grounds and gardens breathtaking. Miss Edwards was very particular in her care of each guest room. She continued to restore and refine Blinkbonnie with fine linens, beautiful china, and period lamps and figurines. The staff were all well trained and encouraged to feel like part of the family. All the MacDonald buildings were eventually converted to guesthouses, as well as the adjacent carriage houses and cottages.

Sadly, Miss Edwards' determination to maintain this level of excellence finally cost her the hotel, because she did not have the means to maintain it after her retirement from teaching. Blinkbonnie was sold in 1957, divided into private homes, and was passed to many successive owners. It became a dark shadow of its former self.

Only Charles remained a witness to the sad changes. Did Rebecca Edwards choose to stay as well? Did her years of ownership and love of Blinkbonnie hold her to it?

In 1983, the Seal family purchased the historic inn. Their intent was to restore the nineteenth-century building and property to its former glory.

The restored Blinkbonnie Harbour Inn features fifty units, including whirlpool suites, a bistro restaurant, a pool, and an English-style pub. The convention facilities can accommodate up to 120 people. Derek, the maintenance supervisor, has spent the last thirteen years taking care of the building, the property, and the guests of the inn — and perhaps Charles himself.

"I often hear footsteps and doors opening and closing, and sometimes I can hear a woman singing in the lounge area," said Derek. Of course no one is to be seen.

A few years ago, Derek encountered a man at Blinkbonnie who claimed to be a psychic. According to him, he could sense the presence of a man, a woman, and a little girl. For years, people have acknowledged the presence of Charles MacDonald's spirit. But who could the woman and the little girl be?

Miss Edwards is thought to be the woman, possibly too attached to leave. After all, she put her heart and soul into Blinkbonnie. As for the little girl, no one seems to know.

The third floor of Blinkbonnie has not been used for several years. Water and electricity is shut off to this level. One night after closing time, Derek was making his final rounds of the building when he heard water running. Oddly enough, the sound was coming from the third floor. Derek and a fellow employee, Mark, started up the stairs. Yes, there was water running somewhere on the third floor. How could this be when the water was shut off to this level?

The men soon discovered that the sound was coming from the bathroom. As they stood outside the door the noise stopped. They entered cautiously. The bathtub was full of water. And there was something even more bizarre about the tub full of water — there was no stopper in the drain!

Mark is quite familiar with Blinkbonnie. He grew up across the street from the inn. In the fall of 1985 he started to work there full-time as a bus boy. "I worked as a waiter, night man, bartender, maintenance person, and finally assistant manager. I lived up on the third floor for two years in 1987 to '88. In those days the inn closed down for the winter and I would be the only person residing in the building."

He has much to relate about ghostly activity. "Once, in the middle of the night, I heard this loud crash in the bathroom. I sat up. I decided to check it out. When I entered the bathroom, I discovered the glass globe that covered the ceiling light bulb had crashed to the floor and broken. The light bulb was screwed in and intact. You would have to unscrew it in order for the globe to fall to the floor.

"On another occasion I awoke to the sound of a splash against the window. It sounded like someone had thrown a snowball at the glass. I got up and peeked out the curtain. There was snow on the ground but no footprints."

In 1985, employees of the Federal Health and Welfare Department booked a number of rooms at Blinkbonnie for a holiday. These guests had more in mind than pure relaxation. They brought an Aboriginal psychic with them, intending to conduct a séance. At the time, Mark was working as a bartender. He told me what happened. "The group decided to hold the séance in room 302. They had brought a ouija board with them. During the séance, the psychic saw the figure of Charles MacDonald appear in the room.

"The weirdest thing about this session was when the Native woman saw the ghost of a young girl appear next to her, but the girl was part of their group and still very much alive. The poor girl fled the room and rushed down to where I was at the bar. She was mortified. Did this mean she was going to die? The whole experience was never explained."

Although Mark is no longer employed at Blinkbonnie, he will never forget the unexplained experiences he encountered while working there.

On June 13, 2014, journalist Wayne Lowrie wrote,

> In its most recent incarnation, the Blinkbonnie is part of the Clarion Inn. Its owner had plans to turn it into a restaurant/pub but last month he approached the town hall for a demolition permit. The application was later withdrawn and last week town council voted to put the Blinkbonnie on a list of buildings of historic interest.
>
> The Blinkbonnie is now up for sale, and its future is uncertain.

Charles MacDonald is likely to remain at Blinkbonnie forever. After all, it was his most beloved home. Are any of us likely to find such a suitable place, and if we do, would we want to leave it either?

Grafton Village Inn

~ Grafton ~

A woman searches through empty rooms and narrow hallways in the Grafton Village Inn, looking for a place to rest. She glides up the central staircase and enters the second floor ballroom. Her attention is drawn to a window overlooking the quiet main street. For a brief moment she glances outside before her gaze settles on the windowsill. A tear drops onto a fractured slab of misplaced limestone resting on the ledge. The word *Fran* is visible on the slab. In that moment she fades from sight. The Grafton Village Inn, it seems, has a permanent guest.

Driving east along Highway 2 last summer, I reached the small village of Grafton and first saw the inn. Somehow I knew a spirit haunted that building. I turned around and parked across the road. I crossed the street, opened the front door, and walked in. I promptly asked the first waitress I saw if the place was haunted. "Oh, yes," she replied. "Come with me." Up the stairs we went to look at — a tombstone!

My hunch was right.

At one time Grafton boasted no fewer than six inns. United Empire Loyalists, mainly from Vermont and Massachusetts, settled

In the background is the Grafton Village Inn, or Pepper's Tavern as it was known in 1833. The building in the foreground is the local town hall.

the village around 1798. British and Irish immigrants followed closely behind.

The settlement was known as Haldimand Corners, named after Sir Frederick Haldimand, a Swiss-born citizen who later became governor-in-chief of Upper Canada from 1778 to 1786. In March of 1832 the village was renamed Grafton in honour of the former home of resident John Grover from Massachusetts.

In November 1833, the *Cobourg Star* newspaper printed an excerpt from a letter written by a visitor to the Grafton Village Inn.

> Our respected host, Mr. Pepper, late of Grovers Inn has taken possession of this beautiful new establishment, the Mansion House. A sign has just been elevated displaying the British Arms in bold relief under which are emblazoned the national emblem. His table we found well supplied with substantials, not forgetting the luxuries which have ever distinguished it.

John Arklands purchased the inn in 1835 and operated it until 1855, when it was purchased by Benjamin Brown. Three years later Brown severed a portion, fifty-eight by fifty-eight feet (nineteen by nineteen metres), from the hotel lot and sold it to the Municipal Council of Haldimand for the township building site.

In 1892 Michael Mulhall bought the inn and he raised a family of twelve children there. He severed the west side of the property for the site of Haldimand Telephone System. The Mulhalls sold the establishment in 1921 and it went on to have several owners. During this time the hotel fell into disrepair.

In 1988 Peter and Camilla Dalglish purchased the inn and embarked on major renovations three years later. Their dream was to restore the Grafton Village Inn to its former glory. The couple hired Mark Kieffer to begin the renovations, which continued for five years. Mark's objective was to give the building a more open and spacious interior. The main floor was restored to its original design, with the trim and mouldings accurate reproductions of the originals.

During these renovations marvellous discoveries came to light. Old coins, dating from as early as 1814, were found, as well as an assortment of tools. This was when "Fran's" gravestone was discovered in the basement, where it had been used as a corner foundation support. A fragment was placed on a windowsill upstairs, and not long after the renovations were completed Fran made her presence known.

A portion of Fran's headstone, discovered in the basement of the Grafton Village Inn.

Lynn Maclean has worked at the inn for the past three years. Does she believe in ghosts? "I am normally the type of person to have to see before I believe. However, there are things that happen here that you cannot explain, like doors unlocking on their own."

Fran seems to become active at night after the inn is closed. The problem is that she never locks the door upon her return. Wine glasses that hang above the bar drop and break on their own. Lights go off and on by themselves.

Lynn is not the only employee who believes Fran exists. The chef, Terri Hubbs, added, "I believe in spirits. There are many things happening here that have no logical explanation. Here at the inn the doorbell rings whenever someone enters the building. This is part of our security system. Yet you can find the door open during business hours without having heard the bell.

"Our security system would wake the village up if it went off and yet once in awhile you will discover the side door open and no alarm ringing."

It would seem the alarm system is not ghostproof.

Terri has never seen Fran but she has heard her. "I can hear the rustling of a dress on the stairs, yet no one is visible."

The washrooms for the inn are located in the basement. Apparently Fran frequents the ladies' room. Terri said, "We had to disconnect the electric hand dryer in the women's room. It wouldn't stop running."

When the walk-in fridge was installed, one worker had the fright of his life. "The man who was installing the compressors felt something or someone touch him on the shoulder. Of course there was no one there," said Terri.

Jackie, the assistant manager, has heard her name called when no one was there to call it.

Another employee, Marilyn Popert, who has worked at the inn for the past few years, has had her own share of experiences. Marilyn spends a great deal of time in the basement doing the laundry. She is quite accustomed to Fran's presence there. "I spend hours in the basement. I don't even realize any more that I am talking aloud to her. The lights often flicker off and on when I am downstairs. Yet there is such a sense of peace when she's around."

Marilyn recounted the plumber's experiences, "When he was working on the pipes they would begin to rattle at the other end of the building. No one was in that area of the basement at the time."

On another occasion the heat became quite intense from the boiler and no one could adjust the temperature.

"People are very intrigued about the story of Fran. One resident has said we need to convince her that she is lost and needs to be directed on her way," said Marilyn.

It seems this corner of land, this inn, the cemetery just behind it, the millpond, and the tombstone in the hall window, have a lot of spirit activity. Could any connections be made? Could Fran's full name and history be discovered? There are more questions than answers.

I decided to ask a close friend of mine, another Fran and a well-known Scottish seer, to join me. Sheelagh Fran Gunn is a very gifted person. Her ability to hear and see what others cannot is remarkable. I believe she even has the power to call forth the wind.

We visited the inn in mid-August. Sheelagh went immediately upstairs to view the tombstone on the windowsill. She touched the stone and knew, "Francis Marie was her name. She died in December of 1837. Another individual was buried with her. I am getting the initial G. His name might have been Grant or Graham."

We had some lunch before touring the entire building. As we sat down at the table my attention was drawn to the window. A worker was shovelling earth from a new trench at the back of the old municipal structure next door. I knew the man had made a discovery. He looked shocked and drawn. I excused myself to ask him about it.

"Have you found anything?" I asked.

"Bones," he said.

"Where?"

The man replied, "In the trench, but now they're in that pile of soil."

I was excited, but horrified. Had he actually dug up a grave while Sheelagh and I were looking for ghosts? What a macabre coincidence!

Then he shouted, "Wait a minute. I just found more bones right here in the wall of the trench."

At that moment his boss came around the corner of the building. He asked us what was going on and we showed him the bones and indicated

The Grafton Village Inn as it looks today, after renovations.

the nearby cemetery. The poor man turned pale. I suggested that he keep all the bones together and notify the proper authorities. With that I returned to the inn and joined Sheelagh on the tour. Although I was shaken by the discovery of bones, she was strangely indifferent.

In the basement Sheelagh moved slowly. "I can sense her presence here. She is very close to the old doorway, which is situated not too far away from where her gravestone was discovered.

"She is not a lost soul. She can't leave even if she wants to! She is bound to the property. She is content to be where she is. There is some connection to a child who was drowned on the property.

"We need to go outside into the backyard. She is leading us."

We walked toward a grove of lilac near the building. Sheelagh saw Fran, the ghost, and described her to me because I could see nothing.

"Fran is between thirty and forty-two years of age. She has brown hair and is wearing a long dress and jacket. Her dress is grey with shades of lilac or violet trim. She is standing by her grave."

The outline of two gravesites was apparent near my feet. Back in the building, Sheelagh said, "Most people expect spirits to be troublesome. This is not necessarily true. Fran's spirit actually enhances this business. She is, after all, watching over her home and loved ones."

It seems she is a permanent guest at the Grafton Inn.

The trench turned out to be the final resting place of a cow, which might explain why the discovery of bones didn't elicit a response from Sheelagh.

If you wish to visit Fran, the lady who stands by her grave, the Grafton Inn will welcome you. Grafton is located on Highway 2, east of Cobourg, Ontario.

MacKechnie House

~ Cobourg ~

Elizabeth is lonely, a forgotten child. She is good at hide-and-seek — so good that few people ever see her. She is, in fact, lost to herself; unaware that she is dead. She might seek you out at MacKechnie House, a bed and breakfast establishment in Cobourg, Ontario. If you don't meet Elizabeth, you may encounter a piper or an elderly woman who also share this glorious nineteenth-century Greek Revival manor.

The story of MacKechnie House begins in 1837, when a young man by the name of D'Arcy Boulton relocated to Cobourg and joined his uncle's law firm. In 1843 he persuaded three brothers, Henry, Andrew, and Stuart MacKechnie, to leave Scotland and settle in Cobourg. Captain Wallace, a second cousin, also came along.

At that time Cobourg had a bustling harbour, significant for shipping and immigration. In 1823 the population was a mere 350 citizens. By 1840 it had grown to 3,300.

William Cattermole recorded this description of Cobourg in 1831: "This is a fine and flourishing village, in which many half-pay officers of his Majesty's Army and Navy are comfortably settled. Cobourg is a

The Rose Room. One guest staying in the room felt a spirit tuck them in at night.

handsome and thriving place. It has its stores in abundance, its post office, printing office, with a newspaper, its churches, chapels, wharfs, lawyers, blacksmiths, inns and innkeeper; hatters, shoe makers, and every convenience."

Cobourg featured one hundred and fifty dwellings including twenty stores, three taverns, two schools, a post office, an apothecary, three surgeons, a coach and wagon factory, three furniture warehouses, two brickyards, and several mills on the outskirts of the village.

Upon his arrival in 1843 Stuart MacKechnie purchased a gristmill and piece of property to the west of downtown Cobourg. There he built a sizeable solid-brick, "temple form" Greek Revival-style home. The front porch and double French doors at the main entrance displayed Regency-influenced architecture.

In 1845 the MacKechnie brothers, along with Captain Wallace's son, Sinclair, formed a partnership and constructed a huge woollen mill on the site of the gristmill that Stuart had originally purchased. They called their business Ontario Woollen Mills, and it quickly became the largest woollen mill in British North America. By 1856 the mill was producing 800 metres a day and employing 200 people. The MacKechnies enjoyed considerable prosperity.

In 1853 Stuart became the mayor of Cobourg, but he only served for a period of four months before his untimely death at the age of thirty-six. His widow, Anna Maria Barbara Poore, the daughter of English baronet Sir Edward Poore, was left to manage the estate.

As for the remaining MacKechnie brothers, fortunes come and go. Despite the efforts of the mill manager to maintain production and profit, the business faltered and the Bank of Montreal foreclosed in 1856. The MacKechnies moved on to other things.

Anna Maria Poore MacKechnie expanded the MacKechnie estate to suit her own needs. In the early 1850s she had another wing added to the north side of the house and there she established a sizeable library. Today it serves as a library and dining area.

In 1862 Anna Maria sold the home to Sheriff James Fortune and his wife, Alice. It was during this period of ownership that the estate became known as Mount Fortune. The location dictated the name. The house stood virtually alone on a high piece of land overlooking the town of Cobourg. Lake Ontario was only a short distance to the southeast. The elevation of the land is no longer what it was in the 1860s, but the inhabitants could indeed look down from the "Mount." The Fortunes also increased the size of the house. An extensive addition at the back is the kitchen today.

The sheriff oversaw the operations of the gaol and other community matters until his untimely death in 1864, of Bright's disease at the early age of fifty-one. Rumour indicated some sort of political scandal, and certainly his financial arrangement with his wife was very unusual for the time. The deed to the house and property was only in his wife's name. Obviously the sheriff wanted to protect his property from his financial dealings.

In 1866, shortly after the beginning of the Fenian raids in Niagara, an infantry battalion associated with the Cobourg Militia was billeted behind the MacKechnie house. The Fenian Brotherhood was a society of Irishmen who sought to force the British to give Ireland its freedom. Many Irish-Americans inhabiting the United States near the Canadian border had banded together to attack British-controlled soil. The fear of Fenian attacks continued for five years. For part of the time the MacKechnie house served as an officers' mess. Among the soldiers billeted there was a piper.

The MacKechnie Estate.

Alice Fortune sold the estate in 1869 and the home changed hands several times before Cathryn Thompson and Ian Woodburn bought MacKechnie house from Arnold Burgis in 1993. They moved in with their son, Rory. By then the house was in a state of disrepair and every room was full of heirlooms and boxes of Burgis' possessions. Arnold Burgis had been living in this spacious home alone since the death of his mother.

Ian specializes in restorations and renovations. Cathryn was a business executive in need of a change. A bed and breakfast and catering enterprise seemed the perfect solution. They had a brochure printed.

> Built for Upper Canada settler Stuart MacKechnie in the grand and glorious Greek Revival style, MacKechnie House is the finest remaining example of this type of monumental domestic architecture in the Cobourg area …
>
> The MacKechnie House ghost dates from around the same time (mid-1800s), and local rumour spins tales of a Highland Infantry Company Bagpiper's untimely demise. Duty-conscious to the end (and beyond, it seems!) the only wailing he indulges in is that of his

pipes, and modern encounters with this shy fellow, though delightful, can be sporadic.

However, a reluctant ghost is no reason to put off your visit to Cobourg. By the time you've seen all there is to see in this history- and event-packed corner of Northumberland County, you'd probably just sleep through his nocturnal perambulations anyway!

When Cathryn first moved into the home she had no idea it was haunted. In fact, she had never been exposed to any unexplained spirit activity. "I am not extremely sensitive to spirits. I didn't have an experience until I moved here.

"During the first year we experienced something very unusual. One day a friend and her seven-year-old daughter were sitting in the kitchen. We were chatting away when suddenly her daughter pointed toward the library and said, 'Who is the little girl?' We didn't know what she was talking about. We couldn't see anything."

On three separate occasions, psychics who were staying in the house reported the existence of three spirits in the home, an old woman, a little girl named Elizabeth, and a bagpipe-playing soldier. According to one

A Scottish bagpiper, who was billeted here back in 1866, is still seen on the stairwell.

psychic, Elizabeth longs to play with other children. She is seldom seen because she doesn't want to frighten anyone. Elizabeth lives in the attic, a prisoner of her own world.

At the top of the stairs to the right of the landing is the Rose Room. This is where Mrs. Burgis is said to have died. Could she be the elderly spirit? When Cathryn first began decorating this room she felt the need to choose wallpaper with roses. She even went a step further and had a dried rose framed to hang in the room. The bedspreads also reflect the rose theme. Cathryn is not attracted to roses. In fact, she had no idea why she felt compelled to decorate in this manner. She later discovered that roses just happened to be Mrs. Burgis' favourite flower.

There is a cold spot in this room a short distance from the bed. Guests often complain about feeling a draft in this one area of the room. According to Cathryn there is a reason for this. Near the end of her life Mrs. Burgis was quite ill and bedridden. The nurse staying with her said she tried to get out of bed because she thought that someone had come for her. Mrs. Burgis rose from her bed and stepped forward to meet a man who only she could see. Then she collapsed and died.

Guests staying overnight in the Rose Room report a cold spot near the table and chairs.

Some people who have stayed in this room have told Cathryn that they could never get warm, even in the summertime. One overnight guest said they felt the spirit tucking them in at night.

Cathryn has to smooth out the blankets on the bed almost every day. It's as if someone lays there on a daily basis. People often complain about the loss of personal items when they stay there. They blame it on forgetfulness or their partner, who they feel certain has placed it somewhere else. Then just when they give up, the item reappears right where they know they left it.

One day Cathryn was about to place a phone call. She carefully took one earring off and placed it on the table before lifting the receiver to her ear. After a lengthy conversation she put the phone down and reached for her earring. It was gone! "Many things go missing, such as clothing. I have lost a skirt, a belt, and some jewellery. These belongings have not yet returned."

Ian often still spends his weekends restoring areas of the house. The disappearance of tools is also not an uncommon occurrence. One day their son Rory asked his dad to hook up the video machine. Ian recalls what happened. "I needed a pair of pliers to do the job. I remember placing the pliers back in the tool box after the job was completed. The next day they were gone. I looked everywhere. Three days later I walked by the video machine and there they were right in front of it, in plain view on the floor."

When asked if he believes in ghosts Ian's reply is, "My mother had just died. I was sitting alone in the living room and I could sense a strong presence. I knew I was not alone in the room. That was it."

One morning a guest named Joanne complained over breakfast about not getting much sleep the night before. Cathryn explains, "Joanne told me a little girl and an elderly woman visited her during the night in her room. Joanne had asked them not to show themselves although she could hear them speak. Joanne said the girl, Elizabeth, was twelve years old. At first Elizabeth told her that she had been dramatically murdered in the house. However, she later said she had died of an illness. She said she was waiting to leave. It was Elizabeth and the elderly woman who told her there was another spirit in the house."

That other spirit could be the Scottish bagpiper who apparently was billeted here back in 1866. Cathryn says, "People who have lived around Cobourg for a number of years and as children played in the house can vividly recall hearing his music. A number of people I have met claimed to have seen him."

Sarah, a lifelong Cobourg resident, attended a birthday party in the house back in the late 1960s and this is what she saw: "There was a group of us playing on the second floor of the home. We had never heard of ghosts before. For whatever reason, I looked up at the staircase that leads to the third floor. I caught a glimpse of the back of a man from the waist down just as he was turning the top of the stairs. I saw one leg. He was wearing a black shoe and a kilt. I knew it was a kilt because I was a highland dancer at the time. The kilt was the Black Watch tartan with dark blue and green and a bit of yellow. I wasn't the only one who saw him. We rushed up the stairs but there was nothing there."

Little is known about this piper or his reason for remaining in the house. Cathryn and Ian have never seen him or heard his music.

In December 1997 Cathryn did encounter one of the spirits. "Back then I was usually rising about four a.m. to begin my catering work. I had one businessman who was a guest staying for the week. He rose for breakfast promptly at seven-fifteen a.m. I always made sure I had coffee ready before he arrived in the kitchen. This particular morning I slept in. I awakened at six-thirty a.m. to the sound of footsteps going down the stairs. Thinking it was him I rushed down to the kitchen to hit the switch on the coffee percolator. No one was there, but someone had helped me out: just as I entered the kitchen the coffee percolator started to drip. I stood there in shock."

On yet another occasion Cathryn was astounded by the generosity of the spirits. "I always know how much money I have in my wallet. On this particular day I was going out for lunch with some friends. I knew I had two five-dollar bills in my wallet. Before reaching the restaurant I gave one five-dollar bill to my son before dropping him off. I then stopped at a convenience store and spent the other five dollars. During lunch a musical group entertained us. I decided to have the waiter deliver five dollars and a request to one of the players. I pulled my wallet out and to my amazement discovered the five dollars was gone. I made a fuss about missing this money. I couldn't believe it. Then I realized on the way home, after picking up my son, that I had spent the money at the variety store. Feeling quite foolish with myself I drove home. There at the top of the basement stairs was a soaking-wet five-dollar bill. I then remembered the psychics saying the spirits were there to help me."

Cathryn and Ian renovated the north wing at the back of the house into an apartment that they rent out. A previous tenant once borrowed two books from Cathryn. After she had read the books they were returned. Cathryn remembers placing them on her desk. One day she noticed that one book had disappeared. A short time later her tenant discovered the missing book back in her apartment standing upright on the floor.

The same tenant often complained about missing her clip-on sunglasses. Each time she would have to go out and buy another pair. Then one day the missing sunglasses appeared. Three pairs of sunglasses, all clipped together, were discovered on a shelf.

MacKechnie House hosts many celebrations. One evening Cathryn catered for a woman who wanted to celebrate her fiftieth birthday by holding a séance in the house. She hired a psychic and invited eighteen people to attend.

According to Cathryn, "It was a strange experience. They held the séance in the library and dining room. Holding hands they waited and waited. Then someone spoke, 'There is something in the basement.'"

Cathryn said, "I believe this. I have seen a pink light or beam travel by me. I can also feel someone standing behind me. At the top of the basement stairs you often get the feeling that someone is walking by." This is the same place where the $5.00 bill mysteriously appeared.

When it comes to spirits one never knows what will happen next. This was true for Cathryn one day last year when she went shopping for antiques in Port Hope. "I was in Port Hope visiting an antique shop on the main street. The woman who owns the store said to me, 'Have you seen the ghost?'

"I replied, 'No, but we understand we have three ghosts. One of them is a little girl, another an elderly woman, and there is a bagpiper.

"I then said to the woman, 'I wonder if the elderly woman is Mrs. Burgis?'

"Then the lady said to me, 'My dead grandmother is with me.' I said, 'Oh yes, I feel that way about my grandmother, too.'

"The woman was looking at me with tears in her eyes. 'You don't understand. My grandmother is talking to me right now. And Mrs.

Burgis has asked my grandmother to ask you to give her permission to leave this plane.'

"I was at a loss for words. I said, 'All right.'

"I came home and went to the room where Mrs. Burgis had died. I then addressed her. I said 'You are more than welcome to stay but if you want to go, please do so.'"

It would seem she didn't go. Just a week later a guest staying in the Rose Room was hugged. During the night the guest felt a coldness around her shoulders and neck. It felt as though someone was embracing her. Was it Mrs. Burgis?

When did Elizabeth arrive and why did she stay? How did the bagpiper die? Why did Mrs. Burgis not leave with the male figure at her bedside? Who or what is the presence in the basement?

Elizabeth and Mrs. Burgis seem to have a friendship, or at least communication with one another. Is this common phenomenon in the spirit dimension? Other ghosts at other sites seem oblivious to one another. Does this mean they were connected in life or is this just another coincidence?

At least Elizabeth has someone to talk to! Maybe you should pay her a visit.

The Orchards

~ Prince Albert ~

In *Haunted Ontario* I alluded to the haunting of my previous home. This is the full story:

The Orchards is a beautiful house in Prince Albert, Ontario, built by James McBrien in 1870 for his bride. McBrien was the first inspector of public schools for the province of Ontario under Egerton Ryerson. He built his home in the Cape-Cod tradition of white clapboard with green shutters and trim. It had a magnificent cabriole veranda and two-storey summer kitchen with servants' quarters upstairs.

The McBrien family was a well-educated, artistic, musical, and spiritually active family. There was one "black sheep," a troublesome son named Sydney who did things like sell the family chickens for money to buy himself a drink or two.

All in all they were an upstanding family, well-respected in the community; folks smiled when Major-General James H. McBrien Junior rode his horse to town to get the mail. James McBrien Junior spent some years in the North West Mounted Police and saw service in the South African War. From there he went to Australia on military service and the

Heartland, or the Orchards, the former home of the McBriens.

Military College at Cambridge, England, where he studied military technique. During the First World War he was appointed to the general staff. He was later made chief of staff at Ottawa, becoming the head of affairs in the Department of Militia and Defence. He retired as the head of the Royal Canadian Mounted Police. His sister Julia McBrien was a concert pianist who travelled to Persia and California. Another sister, Elizabeth, produced art that hangs in the National Art Gallery.

The Orchards remained in the family for a hundred years. In 1970 the two remaining McBrien sisters sold it to Joe and Dolores Victor, who sought a place to hold Gurdjieffan group-work intensives. The Victors shared a toast and sealed a deal with the elderly McBrien sisters. The spiritual history of the home was to continue.

When the Victors moved in they discovered that the house had been left completely as they had first seen it. No furniture had been removed;

even the clothes were hanging in the closet. The pictures on the walls and the sherry glasses the McBrien sisters had used were still on the coffee table. It was incredible.

There was a hundred years of family history — a penny-farthing bicycle, a beautiful harp, decades of period furniture and valuables, a three-holer outhouse in the back, and an elaborate old cookstove in the summer kitchen. Dolores made herself right at home and it wasn't too long before she discovered they were not "alone." The elderly sisters had moved to a nursing home, but someone was still there.

Among the things that happened was the constant slamming of the hall door that joined the house to the summer kitchen. It would slam in Dolores's face, it would slam her in the back. Her bed would shake as if it was trying to fall apart. She was a strong woman, a spiritualist and not easily intimidated — ever! She told her unseen housemates "This is my house now. You live here if you like but leave me alone. Stop slamming doors and shaking beds. I've had enough!"

Surprisingly, the mischievous poltergeist activity abated. Although Dolores tore down the summer kitchen and added a weaving studio, she left the main house as it was. She would say, "The studio is mine; the main house is 'their' period."

Eventually, Dolores' mother Susy came to live with the Victors. Susy was getting on; she had a hard time getting around and liked to make trouble. She also smoked. The spirits didn't like that — or did they? Did the spirit want the cigarettes gone, or did it want the cigarettes? Sydney had been the family rebel, after all. Susy could never keep a pack long enough to smoke it. The cigarettes would simply disappear and would usually turn up in another room.

In 1976 I met Dolores Victor. I was a journalist/entrepreneur with my own magazine and I had gone to interview her for a feature article. I discovered an intriguing, delightful, and somewhat awe-inspiring woman. Together we, along with some others, gave birth that year to a school for artistic and cultural pursuits which we called "The School of Creativity." We taught Tai Chi, poetry, watercolours, drama, and calligraphy. In 1983 courses in spirituality, healing techniques, and Aboriginal studies were added and the name was changed to the J. McBrien School of Creativity.

Delores often spoke about the frustration she experienced in the early seventies when she was redecorating. The painters quit because the lid kept being put on the paint can and their tools would go missing unless she stayed right there with them. The man repairing the stairs constantly had his hammer taken downstairs or upstairs when he wanted it left on the step. A man was frequently seen rocking in a chair on the verandah. A woman in a long gown "lived" in the blue room at the top of the stairs, which remained undecorated and unrepaired until 1980. She was also seen walking in the backyard. She resembled the photographs of Julia McBrien.

I had occasion to stay over one evening. It was my first encounter with the active spirit world there. (Little did I realize that it would be here that I would meet my life partner, Allanah, here that I would come to live, here that I would begin my career as a writer, and here that I would find material for my book about haunted Ontario). That first night I was horrified. This stately old home certainly looks the part the house in a ghost movie. Reminiscent of a Southern plantation estate, the Orchards was and still is the most awe-inspiring and architecturally divine structure to have been built in the village of Prince Albert.

That particular night Dolores had directed me to spend the night in the upstairs bedroom on the right-hand side of the hall in the front of the house. No one else was living on the second floor at the time. I remember slipping under the covers and drifting off to sleep. It seemed so peaceful. In the night I had what I thought was a vivid dream. I saw a group of people walking down the second floor hallway carrying a coffin. One member of the party was dragging his leg. It spooked me. The next morning I related the dream to Dolores. She nodded knowingly, so I questioned her. She told me that my dream was not a dream, it was something that had actually taken place there in another time. What I had witnessed was the funeral of James McBrien. The gentleman who was dragging his leg was his brother, Sydney. Sydney had injured his leg in an accident many years before.

Allanah lived with Dolores Victor from 1979 to 1993, first with her husband, John, and her their children, Jeremy and Sarah, and after 1986 with me. She has a long account of unexplained activity in the house.

"I first moved to 350 Simcoe Street in 1979. I had experienced paranormal activity there prior to that, when I helped to run an antique store there from August 1977 to 1979. Cigarettes would always go missing.

"One day in 1978 I visited my mentor-friend Dolores, because I was in a very saddened state. She had an appointment in the city, but said I was welcome to stay there as long as I wished. At that time she lived there alone. Five of us, in those days, gathered there in an alcove of the studio each morning for meditation and once a week for spiritual readings. I chose to stay there in the alcove to console myself. The tears flowed, but eventually it seemed more sensible to pray for help and I did. Almost immediately there was a 'presence' that filled the space, a presence of peace and love and comfort unlike anything I had ever encountered. I sat there for some undetermined length of time before I went on about my day and, in fact, my life.

"In 1979 it seemed that whenever I was alone in the house I would be followed by a heavy, persistent energy that almost felt menacing. The following year something sat on me one night in bed and made it very difficult to breathe. Dolores suggested I send the presence packing by repeating the Lord's Prayer and telling it to go. It took three repetitions but whatever it was, it did leave.

"Objects on the refrigerator in the studio kitchen flew off on a regular basis and came close to hurting people many times. At one time that had been the location of a set of stairs to the second floor of the summer kitchen. Maybe spirits walk there still.

"In 1984 and 1986 I 'saw' James McBrien Junior standing in full-dress RCMP uniform on the landing above the studio. Other people have also seen him there. At that time I had not seen any photos of him, but when we bought the home in 1989 we found many old McBrien photo albums. I was astounded to find that he was exactly as I had seen him.

"Dolores passed over in March, 1989. Four of us bought the house and rented out rooms to meet the high monthly overhead. One evening tempers flared and the tension was high. We all retired at about ten o'clock. I was awakened by a loud, hollow, humming drone, sort of musical in tone, at eleven p.m. It could have been a sound in the pipes and I set out to investigate. To my surprise the sound existed in our bedroom, the laundry room below, and the bathroom above, but could not be heard anywhere else in the house. I awakened someone else, Iris, and together we proceeded to 'sit in the sound.' The sound was in a vertical column that penetrated the house, approximately one meter in diameter (three feet). Within the column you could not hear yourself think, it was so loud; outside the column it was still a loud, audible sound; in the hall outside the room it was not possible to hear it at all. We could not understand the phenomenon but felt that it was not threatening. We sat in it until it stopped. It lasted one hour exactly. To my knowledge it has never happened again. I have since read that this is a phenomenon that can occur where two ley lines intersect. Ley lines are magnetic lines that exist within the body of the earth and conduct current for the planet. Where they cross there are power points and phenomena occur such as power surges, trees growing in spirals, and other unusual growth patterns.

"In 1990 a friend and I were talking in the upstairs hall during an electrical storm. I was tired and we sat down for our conversation. We had no more than sat down when a round ball of light, about thirty centimeters (fifteen inches) in diameter moved in through the window, 'rolled' through the air down the hall, and passed through the other end with no visible effect on the house.

"We had a friend do a spirit cleansing of the house in 1991 because it was a worry for some members of the household. We were told that the spirits might go or stay as they were free to decide for themselves. I saw James McBrien at least twice more before we moved in 1993 but most of the other activity seemed to settle down. There was still a problem with articles disappearing and reappearing as well as almost audible conversations and other sounds in the hall.

"Our dogs never did go upstairs unaccompanied, and my daughter, Sarah, preferred to have a pet for company and a lock on her door."

Music can be an expression or ordered movement of the forces of a world with which we rarely come in contact. Some spiritualists believe that all thought expresses itself through sound. People hear this sound as a lovely yet indescribable series of ever-changing chords, akin to the sound of harps or pipes. Angels are considered to be one class of spirit who are devoted to music and habitually express themselves in this way. Hindus believe in musical spirits called gandharvas, and they say that the man whose soul is in tune with music will attract the attention of angels and draw himself into connection with them. Famous composers such as Bach, Beethoven, Mendelssohn, Handel, and Mozart could hear this sound. Some of them spoke of hearing the whole of a grand oratorio, a stately march or a noble chorus in one resounding chord.

"My first experience of sound from the spirit world came in the mid-1990s, when I made a conscious choice to leave southern Ontario and move north to a secluded home in nature. Here I felt that I could be more aware and listen to the sounds of other kingdoms. One morning I awakened to the sound of music. My first thought was that someone had turned the radio on, although this was never a common practice. Then I tuned into the sound. Truly, the best way to describe it was 'heavenly.' Although it was faint it seemed to be coming from the second floor of the house. No one lived in that part of our home. The music was like a chorus of instruments and then it vanished. It may have lasted five or ten minutes.

"I still hear it periodically, always in the early morning hours; sometimes someone else might hear it. It stopped for a period when we were doing construction but last year it returned. It seems as though the music comes in late evening or early morning. Spiritualists believe this musical manifestation highlights the vivid and glowing life around you.

"My personal feelings about our old home are that the McBrien family were attached to this magnificent home and to the high spiritual energy. The crossed ley lines made interdimensional activity a much greater possibility."

Today the home is in private hands. It once again houses an extended family and is yet again the home of "spirits" — the new owners have a minister among them.

The University of Toronto
~ Toronto ~

In the Norman Archway of University College lovers meet in the twilight. In that darkened passageway to Croft Chapter House they share their fiery passion. No notice is taken of the place itself, of the axe-carved doorway. In another time a star-crossed lover wielded his axe at a different pair of lovers. He might still be lurking there.

The downtown University of Toronto campus is haunted by more than one lost soul. Among the ghosts who haunt the campus is a sentinel who keeps the light on in the Soldiers' Tower. Since the 1930s, when a workman fell to his death from the tower, a light has been reported in one of the windows of the Memorial Room. Glenn Oldford, a student and tour guide, pointed out, "Security guards working here feel very uncomfortable. One guard heard someone sneeze, but no one was around. An old man has also been seen in the main hall of Hart House." Some people believe the man could be the caretaker Robert Beard, who spent his life working at the university.

However, the strangest tale of all emerges from the grisly murder at University College in September 1858. In 1857–58 talented European stone masons sculpted gargoyles, cloisters, balustrades, and buttresses on the exterior of the building. These Gothic Revival architectural trimmings highlight the mysterious. You might think that at any given moment one of these gargoyles could move — so many eyes watching from above. A life force stares hauntingly from each stone creation.

Paul Diabolos, a young Greek, and Ivan Reznikoff, an older burly Russian, were two of the stonemasons who worked on University College. Ivan was deeply in love with a young woman named Susie. Her father, a British upper-class businessman, disapproved of their union. The lovers kept their affair a secret. They planned to marry when the college was complete.

Ivan had forsaken his cherished vodka for many months to save for his married life with Susie. They had accumulated $500 in her bank account. But something was not quite right. Ivan brooded darkly over Susie's lack of commitment. He had witnessed Paul and Susie exchanging "looks." Was there something there? Rage and jealousy began to build inside him.

A close friend of Ivan's urged him to leave Susie and find a good Russian wife. He invited Ivan to meet him at dusk by the bench near the maple tree across from Croft Chapter House.

Ivan met his friend. James Louden describes what happened next in his book *Studies of Student Life* (1928): "We'll hide inside the little corridor close to that gargoyle where you worked today. See that bench that leans against the trunk? T'is vacant now, but watch it closely, and thou shalt see two lovers sit there arm in arm, as the shadows grow more dense beneath the friendly maple tree."

As the moon rose two figures did appear, Susie and Paul. They were entangled in each other's arms — and in a web of deceit. Ivan watched and fumed with rage.

Susie thought she heard something. She and Paul went to investigate, arm and arm, toward the archway. Paul struck a match. Although Ivan and his friend hid in the shadows, Paul had seen Ivan. He decided to play to Ivan's anger.

The next day the two men worked apart. But it was only a matter of time before things would come to a head. At the end of the workday Ivan waited by the bench. Hearing a laugh he spun about to find Paul leaning on the parapet, taunting Ivan from the corridor. Paul had a dagger. Ivan grabbed the axe on the bench and charged the archway. Unable to draw his dagger in time, Paul shielded himself from Ivan's attack. Paul narrowly escaped the blow of the axe, which struck the door. The blows rained upon the door and the frame. Paul escaped through the door as the axe struck deep, becoming embedded in the oak.

Paul flew down the hallway and up the stairs, through a swinging door of glass, and then he slipped. Ivan was upon him. Again Paul narrowly avoided calamity and was off again, up more stairs. James Louden adds, "At the top of this narrow flight of steps there is a sudden turn toward the east and half a dozen steps lead to the upper landing from which the main steps of the tower ascend. At the angle of the western wall, just at the top, Diabolos, with dagger upright in his hand, waits for his foe."

As Ivan approached, Paul leapt out and his dagger found its mark. With a groan, Ivan dropped dead to the floor.

Paul knew what to do. Beyond the tower door lay the ideal resting place for Ivan. The well beneath the tower steps would make the perfect grave. He would never be found! Paul dragged the body inside and with the aid of a match he peered into the darkness of the well below. He threw Ivan head first down the twenty-metre (sixty-foot) well. Paul took the axe from the front door. With Ivan gone, Paul and Susie eloped out west, taking Ivan's savings with them. Ivan would never be heard from again.

Or would he?

Ivan's restless spirit was first seen on the campus in 1866.

In 1890 fire struck University College. In the ashes the skeletal remains of Ivan Reznikoff were discovered. Glenn Oldford tells me, "A chaplain gave Ivan a proper burial in the courtyard of the building. He was buried under a tree."

Somehow, in 1980 Humphrey Milnes, a professor of German, was photographed displaying a human skull, reportedly that of Ivan Reznikoff. As recently at 1996 the skull was reported to still be on display in the principal's office. When was Ivan's head found?

John Louden wrote about a man named John Smith who saw and communicated with the spirit of Ivan. "John is always hazy on the point and remembers nothing except that the ghost intended to put in an appearance every Hallowe'en, or Valentine's Day, he was not sure which. John Smith also has a very vivid description of Reznikoff pounding the table, until the glasses jumped, when he was questioned, in a moment of inadvertence, about the teaching of Greek in the college." Obviously, Ivan was still touchy about a little Greek!

Allen Aylesworth, a former student at the university, later a member of the House of Commons and Senate, encountered Ivan while walking across the campus. He recalled seeing a thickset figure of a man. In the course of the meeting Allen, not thinking him to be anything other than human, invited him back to his student quarters. There they sat by a fire as Ivan told him of his love for Susie and of his death at the hand of Paul Diabolos. He also told Allen about the two faces he and Diabolos carved. He said that his gargoyle was a grotesque face and that Diabolos had carved a smiling one. Ivan said that Diabolos had pointed out that the grotesque face was Ivan and the smiling face was Paul. When Ivan asked Diabolos why, he said that he was laughing at him behind his back!

Allen was shaken. Was this stranger before him really a ghost? Ivan promptly disappeared, his wine half finished.

Years later Allen investigated the story, he learned that Ivan's body had been recovered from the stairwell in the fire of 1890. He also saw the two sculpted faces positioned on the face of the building near the passageway where Ivan first wielded his axe. The door tells its own tale because it is still in place, axe marks and all!

Over the years there have been many sightings of the spirit of Ivan Reznikoff on the campus grounds or in the building. When Ivan is around the lights go on and off.

When Glenn Oldford and I were touring the campus we eventually entered the passageway where Ivan left the axe marks on the door. As Glenn recounted some of the history, Reznikoff's name was mentioned. The lights went off.

At dusk I took some pictures of the gargoyles and the door. I used a flash because the light had gone off. I had no sooner finished than the light came on. I took new pictures. Obviously, he was letting me know that he was still around!

Beware of Croft Chapter alcove for a lovers' secret rendezvous. You might resemble Paul and Susie and Ivan might be awaiting their return. Perhaps that's why he stays on campus.

The Hockey Hall of Fame
~ Toronto ~

They were trustworthy individuals, handling other people's money every day, but they gambled dangerously with their own lives. They worked together at a beautiful old bank at Yonge and Front Streets in Toronto.

First constructed in 1885 during a period of prosperity and optimism about Canada's future, the Bank of Montreal marked the rise of commerce and an age of decadence. In its day it was the largest bank branch in Canada. The building is a florid example of rococo architecture and was designed by the Toronto firm Darling and Curry. It served as the head office of the Bank of Montreal until 1949 and then as a branch office until 1982, when it was closed permanently.

The central hall measures twenty-one metres by twenty-one metres and rises thirteen metres to a stained-glass dome. The dome is the largest of its kind in Toronto. It was constructed by Joseph McCausland and Sons and features twenty-four fanned panels that depict allegorical dragons guarding gold from eagles. Around the outside are cornucopia filled with fruit and flowers. In the centre circles are emblems representing the provinces of Canada.

The detail in the hall is exquisite. The framing of the mezzanine on the west side that once served as the boardroom is incredible. The bank manager's private apartment was located just behind the mezzanine. Outside an octagon reflects the interior, diagonal corner arches. To the left of the south portico a huge stone figure of Hermes stands. He has supported the weight of the building's chimney on his shoulders for all these years. Massive, arched plate-glass windows indicate the size of the interior.

It was the perfect setting for romance to blossom, and blossom it did.

Her name was Dorothy. An attractive woman who worked as a teller in the bank, she was the most popular girl on staff. Her handsome lover was also employed as a teller. They had to keep their liaison a secret. Not only were they co-workers, but he was already married. If anyone suspected their love they could both lose their jobs.

Their fellow workers were starting to smile at them differently. Some of the women quit speaking, as if interrupted, when Dorothy entered the room. And then something snapped. Her lover broke it off — a change of heart — and Dorothy was cast aside. Devastated by his betrayal, she slipped into a state of deep depression. Hurt, humiliated, fearful that her former friends at the bank knew her shame, Dorothy still had to go to work every day.

One morning in March of 1953, she entered the bank at 7 a.m., went up to the women's washroom on the third floor, and remained there for some time.

When he was interviewed by *Toronto Star* journalist Stefan Scaini, Len Redwood, chief messenger for the bank, recalled seeing Dorothy that morning. "It was much earlier than she was expected to be in. She looked pretty rough, probably had had a night out." A night out or a sleepless night?

She returned downstairs for a brief time, and then went upstairs again. Redwood described what happened, "The next thing I heard was a shot."

Dorothy had taken the bank's own revolver and shot herself in the head.

In those days each bank had a least one gun. Employees were expected to shoot it out with robbers.

Dorothy's death sent shockwaves through the employees and, no doubt, her former lover.

Unexplained things began to happen immediately. The lights in the bank would go on and off by themselves. Locked doors were discovered to be wide open.

Redwood admitted, "We all felt something. There was someone watching us but you couldn't see anyone. The cleaning staff became nervous about working in the bank after dark, claiming they heard funny noises. The women refused to use the upstairs washroom, so the bank was forced to build another one in the basement."

Over forty years later, on June 18, 1993, the Hockey Hall of Fame opened the doors of its current home in this magnificently restored Bank of Montreal. The main mission of the organization is to collect and preserve objects and images connected with the game of hockey.

A second objective is public education about the history and rules of play of this great Canadian game. Schools, tourists, and hockey fans alike tour the facilities on a daily basis. Visitors enjoy the many exhibits on display, including the hall of hockey's finest players. In the first year of operation, more that 500,000 people visited the building.

In 1993 William Houston of the *Globe and Mail* wrote, "The new Hockey Hall of Fame in Toronto has just about everything, including a ghost. The ghost is Dorothy and she resides in the restored Bank of Montreal building that is part of the new Hall of BCE Place.

"Over the years, custodians of the bank have heard shrieking and moaning noises coming from the rooms. Items have gone missing or have been moved."

Christine Simpson, who is in charge of publicity at the new Hall says, "If we've misplaced something we say, 'Well, it must be Dorothy.'"

Recently a gentlemen and his young son arrived to tour the hockey exhibits. After proceeding through the lower concourse level they entered the building proper. Directly ahead of them, just to the left, was an elevator; the door was open. The son stood staring fixedly at the elevator doorway as he watched the ghost of a pretty young woman beckon him to enter. Seconds later the door closed and travelled up to the third floor.

For half a century Dorothy has remained behind. She gambled everything for love — and she lost.

Joseph Brant Museum

~ Burlington ~

A mysterious woman appears in the corridor dressed in a white-satin Victorian gown, a veil covers part of her hair. She searches for the door that will lead her to freedom and the person who has the key to that door. Her appearance is captivating but, nevertheless, chilling. Very few people have seen her. One person to whom she has spoken has never fully recovered from the experience. The "Lady in White" is waiting ...

This strange presence walks the halls and grounds of the Joseph Brant Museum in Burlington, Ontario. Most people sense nothing out of the ordinary here. In fact, neither staff nor director admit to the existence of a spirit. Is it denial — or disbelief? A museum is, after all, a storehouse of historical artifacts to educate people about the past, to broaden and expand one's sense of identity in time. Just how much of the "invisible" past can be housed along with it? Just ask the one visitor who has willingly shared an unforgettable, unexplainable encounter that took place twelve years ago in this museum. The experience was so intense that she never returned until this year when she was asked to reveal her story about the Victorian lady in white. What

The Joseph Brant Museum in Burlington.

connection does this have to Joseph Brant's home or to the hotel that once stood on this site?

Our story begins with Joseph Brant (Thayendanegea), a Mohawk leader who, in 1798, was granted 3,450 acres on Burlington Bay by King George III for service to the Crown during the Seven Years' War and the American Revolutionary War. Brant built a home on his property just a few hundred yards to the southwest of the present-day museum. His dwelling was a two-storey house built of timber brought from Kingston by water in 1800. He chose a site at the Head of the Lake overlooking the bay and beyond. He and his wife, Catherine, and their family resided here. In 1807 Joseph Brant died in his home at the age of sixty.

Brant's son, John, was thirteen when his father passed away and he and his younger sister, Elizabeth, continued to live there with their mother. Little is known of their lives over the years that followed. W.L. Stone, biographer of Joseph Brant, believes that Elizabeth and her husband, William Johnson Kerr, were residing in the old mansion in 1837. Apparently, Elizabeth inherited the home when John died in 1832.

In 1845 the Kerrs died, leaving behind four children. One son, W.J. Simcoe Kerr, followed in his father's footsteps and graduated from

Osgoode Hall in 1862 as a lawyer. It was during this time that the Kerrs, for reasons unknown, resided elsewhere and rented the estate and the farm to a Mr. Henry.

On December 17, 1869, Simcoe Kerr moved back to the homestead. A year later he married Kate Hunter. The couple had no children. Simcoe Kerr died on February 18, 1875. A year later his sister also passed away. It was during this period that the estate was sold and the homestead was incorporated as the Brant House, a luxurious summer resort. The house had a verandah that swept two sides and many gables. The interior, according to Clair Emery and Barbara Ford in their book *From Pathway to Skyway*, was turned into a series of individual motel-like apartments and became a popular spot for vacationers. The Halton Atlas of 1877 featured the Brant estate, which at that time sported twenty acres of gardens, croquet lawns, a bowling green, bathing "machines," ice cream parlours, and a dance hall. The proprietor of the establishment was J. Morris.

A.B. Coleman eventually purchased the property and in 1899 began the promotion of a second hotel structure adjacent to the Brant House. On July 2, 1902, the new hotel, named the Hotel Brant, opened its doors to the public. Erected at a cost of $100,000, the Hotel Brant was described as "a spacious building with accommodation for 250 guests."

The hotel was very modern and popular. It had elevators, electric lights, sanitary plumbing, and hot-water heating. This new tourist centre, surrounded by lawns and numerous shade trees, was situated on a high bluff overlooking both Lake Ontario and Hamilton Bay. The hotel's dining room was a massive 900 metres (8,000 square feet) and live music played at mealtimes. Hotel rates started at $2.50 a day. A special feature of the establishment was a roof garden. An early brochure of the hotel advertised golf, tennis, croquet, bowling on the green, bathing, boating, fishing, cycling, driving, pin bowling, billiards, pool, bagatelle, and ping pong. The manager of these many fine amusements was Thomas Hood. The Brant House complex was renamed The Hotel Brant and Annex.

The Hotel Brant was unable to serve alcohol due to its location in the dry part of town. Male guests found this situation quite inconvenient. Mr. Coleman was sensitive to the needs of his guests and thereby resolved to purchase a piece of land across the way and open a country club in the wet section of town to satisfy his thirsty patrons. This building was later remodelled and became known as the Brant Inn. It was destroyed by fire in 1925 and then reconstructed. Famous entertainers such as Sophie Tucker, Ella Fitzgerald, Liberace, Lena Horne, and Benny Goodman were frequent entertainers at the Brant Inn.

In August of 1917 the Hotel Brant and Annex was expropriated by the federal government and remodelled for use as a soldier's hospital. The expansive verandahs were boarded up and remodelled to create wards. Many of the other hotel rooms became operating theatres. The hospital staff resided in the annex. There are no reports to indicate how many soldiers were treated or died there.

In the 1930s the remaining veterans were transferred to Toronto. A short time later the hotel and annex were vandalized and parts of the building destroyed by fire. Eventually the buildings had to be demolished.

Ontario minister of highways T.B. McQuesten was instrumental in the erection of Joseph Brant House. McQuesten recalled visiting the original Brant Annex with his mother as a little boy. He was so impressed with the history of the area that he felt obligated to ensure that a piece of that history be honoured. On May 23, 1942, the Joseph Brant Museum, a replica of Joseph Brant's home, was officially opened. The museum was situated a few hundred yards from the original site. The loading docks of the Joseph Brant Hospital, located to the west, are said to be on the actual site of the hotel and annex.

The first reports of a haunting of Joseph Brant's home were recorded as early as 1873 in the American Historical Record and later recounted in the *Hamilton Spectator*. One visitor shared his experiences within the building during Brant's ownership.

> This venerable structure presents nearly the same appearance as it did ... when Captain Brant, with a retinue of 30 servants and surrounded by soldiers, cavaliers in powdered wigs and scarlet coats and all the motley assemblage of that picturesque era, held his barbaric court within its walls. The rumour was reported to me in good faith by a neighbouring farmer that the Brant House is haunted.

According to Michael Bennett's report in the *Hamilton Spectator*, "Visiting psychics have said the supernatural 'heart' of the building lies in the small third-floor room."

Mr. Bennett also refers to an article that appeared in the *Hamilton Spectator* in 1891. "Grisly find on the Brant property. Investigators digging in a mound discovered the skeleton of a large, male Native. Two ivory rings still pierced his nose and alongside him in the grave lay a tomahawk, pipe and knife."

Who was the person and why was he buried here? Certainly the disturbance and removal of a body from its sacred burial place is often enough to begin a spirit haunting.

Who really haunts the Joseph Brant Museum?

For years the nursing staff on the second and third floors of the Joseph Brant Hospital have witnessed unusual activity in the museum across the way. The nurses have a very clear view and have reported lights going off and on in the rooms on the second floor and in the attic space on the third floor; some have seen an apparition walk by a second-storey window in the middle of the night. Could it be the "Lady in White"?

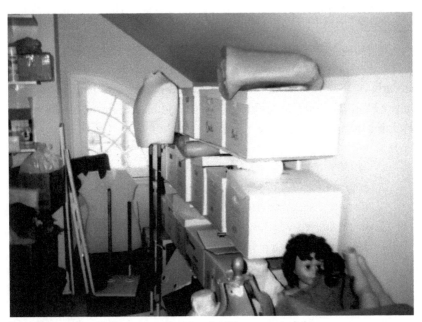

People have seen lights going off and on in this room at night.

In 1987 a group of Burlington Jaycettes met at the Joseph Brant Museum in the evening. Their meeting was to begin at 8:00 p.m. sharp in the room located to the right on the second floor. The upstairs of the museum is comprised of a short corridor at the top of the stairs with a bookcase on the left. Adjacent to the corridor on the right is a large room that faces the hospital and a smaller exhibition room with a glass case on the left. Past this display room is a small hallway leading to an office and a narrow staircase leading to the attic on the third floor.

Mary (not her real name) arrived on time and took a seat just inside the doorway. A male friend was seated beside her. Sometime between 8:00 p.m. and 9:30 p.m. Mary had an unexpected terror of a visitation.

Mary is a middle-aged woman of slight build. She knows more than most people will ever realize. She is a sensitive, a person who attracts the spirits of the deceased. It is this gift of sight that terrifies her when she senses evil. Recently, on a warm spring day, Mary, accompanied by a friend, nervously approached the museum. She did not want to enter the building. She felt fear. Her need to tell her story, to be heard and believed, gave her the courage that she needed. With trembling hands she began her story of what happened that night. She has not stepped foot in the building in all these years since her experience.

On that evening, Mary had been seated facing north, which meant the doorway leading to the corridor was on her right. For some reason her attention was drawn to the doorway. "I looked out the door and there she was, standing in the hallway, looking right at me. She made eye contact with me. She was wearing a white dress with long sleeves. Her dark-brown hair was partially covered by a veil. It almost looked like a wedding dress, but not quite.

"She was just standing there. I heard her plain as plain can be. She was talking to me. I asked a man seated beside me to look. He couldn't see her. She appeared to be in her mid-twenties, not beautiful, but not unattractive either. She was very thin.

"She said 'My name is Eliza. I was born in England in 1847. Don't let my appearance fool you because things are not as they seem.' Then she was gone."

Mary was so frightened that she fled the building.

What has kept Eliza there and what "things are not as they seem?"

Mary saw a female spirit, wearing a white dress, standing outside this door in the hallway.

The museum volunteer co-ordinator at the time, Ann Urquhart, was determined to get to the bottom of the haunting. She left a tape recorder running after the museum closed for the night in order to catch the spirit on tape. In his newspaper article, Michael Bennett explains, "On at least one occasion Ann Urquhart caught sounds she describes as 'the rustling of papers and a cupboard door closing.'"

Mary later said, "I figured out what she meant when she said 'things are not as they seem.' I listened to one tape made by Ann that picked up the sound of coins being dropped on the table. Eliza was a woman of the night."

Michael Bennett surmised, "Speculation is that Eliza was banished from the respectful ground-floor rooms of the old Hotel Brant but greeted her visitors on the second-floor landing where the encounter took place. The attic room where her presence is most felt by those sensitive to such things corresponds to the room where Eliza did her entertaining."

Mary believes the white dress Eliza was wearing was deceiving. She wasn't as pure as the colour white represents. At the time of the sighting the glass display cabinets situated in the room to the right of the corridor housed a collection of Victorian dresses. Mary said, "I could not walk past the cabinets."

Barbara Teatero, the museum director, adds, "One day while I was working at my desk I looked down the hallway and saw two women standing in front of the display case with their hands on the glass. I asked them if I could help them. They replied, 'You have friendly ghosts here.'"

Perhaps Eliza's white dress is in the museum's extensive Victorian collection that is now in storage on the third floor. Perhaps Eliza's world has remained. She is still working in the hotel! Mary certainly wouldn't disagree that Eliza lives in the building. Her experience was real and terrifying. But why terrifying?

"She frightened me. It was how she spoke to me." Eliza's tone of voice carried a menacing force that still remains with Mary today.

Mary remained tense and I felt there was more to her story. "Mary, this isn't the first ghost you have seen, is it?" I asked her.

She hung her head and remained silent. Tears formed in her eyes and streamed down her face. Her friend reached for a tissue. She felt safe enough in the moment to reveal herself. "In 1978 we thought of moving and looked at a house in Burlington. This fairly modern home had been on the market for a long time. For some reason it wouldn't sell. We wondered why but we bought it.

"One day I was in the kitchen preparing lunch when someone touched me. I was the only person in the house.

"We then discovered that the builder of the home had died constructing the home.

"On another occasion I entered the house and there he was, standing in the room. He had reddish-blonde, curly hair and a beard. He was wearing a plaid shirt and jeans, as if dressed for work. I had a picture of Jesus Christ hanging on the wall. I glanced over at the picture and caught him doing the same. We looked at each other and then I knew that it was okay. I called him by his name, Kevin.

"My son never saw him, but did hear his footsteps.

"We lived with this spirit for fifteen years. When we moved from the house I cried."

Still dabbing her eyes, Mary glanced down. In this moment I knew her stories were true. She could judge the intent of the two separate spirits. Kevin was kind and unobtrusive. Eliza generated quite a different atmosphere.

I felt it was time for me to seek out Eliza in the museum. I travelled from room to room taking photographs of every nook and cranny. I snapped several shots of the display case, hoping to catch an image of Eliza in the glass. Then I wandered up the narrow staircase to the attic. I knew she was there. I pondered the story that the museum director shared of an experience she and her sister had in the attic. "My sister and I were up on the third floor putting away costumes in boxes. Suddenly one of the boxes flew up and hit my sister on the shoulder."

Yet when I asked if she believes in ghosts she responded with a hesitant, "No."

As I walked around the attic I tried to imagine what this building was like as a hotel. What other spirits haunted this place? What haunting was the writer referring to back in 1873? Who was the male spirit one psychic spoke about on the first floor? I shot some pictures without incident. Little did I realize what would happen next!

I walked into the corridor on the second floor where Eliza had been seen. A floor-to-ceiling bookcase was situated to the right of me. I decided to check the book collection for historical information about Brant's house and the hotel. An elderly gentlemen was seated in a chair about one metre (three feet) away, working at a desk. His job was to catalogue the library. Gazing up to the third shelf I spotted a book I had written back in 1979. Thinking that I might take a look at it again, I reached up and placed my hand on the book. It suddenly flew off the shelf, along with three others. Two of the other books landed on the floor, while the book I had written, called *Under This Roof*, managed to strike the gentlemen by the desk on the side of the head, knocking his glasses across the hall. What on earth had happened? My attention went immediately to the man, hoping he wasn't hurt. I found his glasses and returned them to him. In his mind, I had caused the accident. I apologized but I knew full well that I had not done the deed. Eliza had shown her hand. There was no way those books could have fallen off the shelf. I had a strong grip on the one book and had not yet pulled on it at all. It happened fast, with great force. I knew she was there and that Mary was right. Eliza is not a kind spirit. I thanked her for making an appearance.

The Joseph Brant Museum is visited by thousands of tourists each year. Most visitors would never know or sense anything out of the norm. They might miss the truly historical exhibit of Joseph Brant's real home and the Hotel Brant that still stands on the property. Obviously some of the characters from those days live on as if nothing has changed. Occasionally someone like Mary discovers them again.

Emma's Back Porch

~ Burlington ~

A figure in a black, lace-topped evening dress devotes her attention to the arrival and departure of her guests. She is the *grande dame* of the Estaminet Restaurant in Burlington and has been since 1919 when Emma and George Byrens purchased an old house that looked out over Lake Ontario on Water Street, now Lakeshore Road. Emma's dream was to open a grand dining establishment and she started with just four tables.

Emma had good taste. She purchased food locally and insisted on the best. When the restaurant was closed, she busied herself in the kitchen preparing preserves for sale. Word of mouth spread and her restaurant was a success.

Over the years the Estaminet grew in size and reputation. It was the place to be seen and to dine. The inscription written Emma's first guestbook testifies to her outlook on life and on business: "A human document rich in contemporary history; a record of the most pleasant side of our times." Later guestbooks are filled with the signatures of dignitaries, politicians, entertainers, and socialites from around the world. These visitors included Liberace, Louis Armstrong, Prime Minister John Diefenbaker, Prime Minister Lester B. Pearson, and Barbara Ann Scott.

One Mothers' Day, Ontario premier Mitchell F. Hepburn, with Mrs. Hepburn and a party of friends, dined there. In May 1931 Viscount Duncannon, son of Canada's new governor-general, Lord Bessborough, had dinner with group of friends. After the meal, the viscount personally congratulated Mrs. Byrens on her excellent establishment.

Emma contributed greatly to the Second World War effort. On one occasion she organized a card party for 400 guests with the proceeds going to the Burlington district branch of the Canadian Red Cross. In 1943, on her seventieth birthday, a gala event was held at the Estaminet to celebrate her life. Emma was not yet ready to throw in the towel, however. She continued as proprietress until she retired in 1952 — and perhaps she has remained longer.

The Estaminet changed hands several times until 1992, when Kalin Johnson and Craig Kowalchuk took over and the restaurant was renamed Emma's Back Porch. It still really does belong to Emma.

Kalin and Craig had a great sense of the history of this site. The area downstairs was turned into a roadhouse bar and lounge, a cozy cottage-like room with a fireplace. They created an elegant semi-formal setting called the Water Street Cookery, where they feature mouth-watering pasta and seafood dishes.

The presence of Emma's spirit was news to Kalin and Craig. They delighted to take it as an omen of prosperity. Emma obviously approves of the new arrangements since she graces the restaurant by standing at one of the windows or walking about the premises. She has been seen many times. Patrons have been tapped on the shoulder or have literally had their menus pulled out of their hands by some unseen force.

When renovations were begun in the early 1990s, workers heard screaming when the ceiling was removed. The renovations eliminated part of the living quarters on the second floor, where Emma and her husband and family once resided.

Three magnificent original stained-glass windows, once visible from the exterior, are now part of the lobby decor. An English sixteen-foot grandfather clock stands in the entrance. A sweeping staircase to the second floor is decorated with many historic photographs and framed pages of Emma's guestbooks.

A psychic session that was held in the building a few years ago resulted in communication with Emma. Craig said, "I knew I was here to take care of her building, and that she would be a good ghost to me after that session."

Kelly Lawlor is the manager of Emma's Back Porch. She does not believe in paranormal activity, but admits to feeling a chill now and then. She does also concede that her staff have had many unexplained experiences in the place. "Emma is mainly seen upstairs in the Water Street Cookery. Staff have seen her walk by the windows of the dining lounge. Customers sitting outside on the lakeside deck have seen Emma gazing out the second-storey windows toward the lake. Most staff members prefer not to venture upstairs after closing time.

"Emma often appears with her white hair in a bun and she is dressed in a black blouse and skirt. One night at 1:30 a.m. a staff member saw her walking around downstairs."

Kelly also feels another spirit exists in the building, that of Emma's son, who apparently drowned at a young age in the lake behind the Estaminet. Perhaps we are witnessing a bizarre reunion.

Some of the staff have been there since Kalin and Craig took over. In the early 1990s the beer fridge was upstairs in the Water Street Cookery. On one occasion a waitress went upstairs for some beer. When she opened the fridge door, much to her surprise, the ghost of a little boy was standing inside, crying. She fled. That same waitress still has a problem with the beer fridge.

"Today we keep the beer in a fridge located in the basement. I have to use all my strength to open and close the fridge door. Two male employees say they have opened the door to have it close on its own."

Another waitress spoke of an experience that happened several years ago. At about 2:30 a.m., a co-worker caught sight of a dark shadow that moved across the downstairs room then quickly exited via the front door.

Journalist Carmela Fragomeni, of the *Hamilton Spectator*, wrote about Emma's Back Porch: "Both Johnson and Kowalchuck talked of their own unusual experiences, and those they heard from their employees, of books flying off the shelf and a large hand-operated salad spinner on the kitchen floor spinning like crazy on its own for about five minutes without decelerating."

Laurel Haber, a long-time resident of Burlington, recalls Emma, "My father's first wife was Emma's niece. Emma did a lot of charity work for the town of Burlington. She really cared about the poor.

"Sunday was the big family day. When you arrived at the Estaminet you entered the front doors and proceeded to a waiting room off to the right called the anteroom. Emma would be there, standing behind a lectern. She was the *grande dame*. She always wore a black evening dress and a silver chain around her neck.

"You would be led down the hall to a huge expansive dining room. I can still recall the decor. There were Chinese lanterns with large red silk tassels hanging from the ceiling. The waiters were dressed in black trousers and white shirts. The waitresses wore French maid outfits. The water was poured from a silver pitcher. This place was Emma's baby. She was welcoming you into her home."

There are indications that two of Emma's children have remained behind. Her young son, who drowned, has not only been seen in the upstairs fridge but also in the basement. Emma had a daughter who also died unexpectedly. She has also been heard from in the basement.

The basement is a very eerie place. There are two secret tunnels from the cellar area. They are covered over now, but one tunnel ran under the street to a house and the second tunnel toward the lake. There are no written accounts of these tunnels, but some historians think they may have been constructed for use during prohibition, since Burlington and the Hamilton Bay were very active in the rum-running trade. They also could have been connected with the Underground Railroad. However, neither of these possibilities could have involved Emma, because the Underground Railroad was before her time and she did not sell illegal liquor during prohibition.

On Halloween of 2001, an investigation was conducted by Canadian ghost expert Patrick Cross and paranormal investigator Carolyn Bassell. Patrick found the ghost of Emma's husband and also discovered the spirits of five happy children playing in the basement. He even managed to photograph the shadowy figures of what appear to be Emma, her husband, George, and one child in the cellar.

Carolyn recalls the first visit to Emma's. "We went to the basement. We picked up a number of spirits there. We heard laughter. I received the name Simon or Steven. The children appear happy and are quite mischievous. There is also the spirit of a man lurking near the tunnel entrance.

"We discovered a cold spot in the kitchen area. Everyone felt quite dizzy. I felt like I was being pulled down. It was here where I contacted a male spirit who had suffered a heart attack. It is quite possible he died here. I was able to send him on his way."

Carolyn was also able to locate Emma in the restaurant. "I picked up the spirit of Emma on the first floor in the log-cabin room. She was sitting on a bench near the stone fireplace. She was wearing a lace-collared, grey dress.

"I noticed some spirit energy near the staircase leading up to The Water Street Cookery. I also located a spirit in the upstairs dining lounge near the seating area. I felt that this spirit had had a long illness and possibly died here."

In December 2001, Carolyn returned once again. "This time I was just outside the kitchen entrance door. There was a gate in the laneway. As soon as I started walking, the gate began to swing back and forth on its own."

There does seem to be a variety of spirit activity at Emma's. In fact, Emma does not seem to have retired from the business. Perhaps your dining experience would be the better for your acknowledgement of Emma, the *grande dame*, when you place your order.

Fort George

~ Niagara-on-the-Lake ~

Musket in hand, a sentry paces the grounds of Fort George, a British fortification on the Niagara frontier. He is waiting for the second American assault. Below, American warships take up their position on the Niagara River. This invasion could begin at any moment. As he turns toward the strategic artillery battery to his right, a thick haze of mist begins to drift in, obscuring his view. When it clears, the soldiers are gone and the battle is over. Strangely dressed people are passing by.

He is a casualty of time, not war.

In 1811, an aggressive America demanded immediate invasion of British North America. Henry Clay, a strong opponent of Great Britain, was confident that an easy victory across the border was as good as done. "I trust I shall not be presumptuous when I state that I verily believe that the militias of Kentucky alone are competent to place Montreal and Upper Canada at your feet."

Clay estimated it would be all over in a short four weeks.

In February of 1812, Congress ordered the organization of a volunteer army of 50,000 men. Four months later the United States declared war on Britain.

Although Great Britain did send some regular military forces to Upper and Lower Canada, their numbers were few in comparison to the American forces. Meanwhile, the presence of the British military on the Niagara Peninsula, under the gallant commander-in-chief Major-General Isaac Brock, fostered a sense of security.

The Jay Treaty of 1794 had given Great Britain two years to vacate their defensive works within the boundaries of the United States. By 1796 they had abandoned Fort Niagara and crossed the Niagara River into Upper Canada. Over the next three years the British built Fort George just outside Newark, now called Niagara-on-the-Lake, the capital of Upper Canada at that time. The fort was constructed on a small rise overlooking the river and the British naval base.

On the morning of October 13, 1812, the famous Battle of Queenston Heights was fought. Major-General Sir Isaac Brock had been busy preparing Upper Canada as well as he could against attack. After he defeated the Americans at Detroit, Major-General Brock quickly left for the Niagara River frontier, where only 1,500 men stood guard against attack.

On the night of October 12th, Major-General Brock rested at Fort George. Just after midnight, the American forces crossed the river at Queenston. Unsure if this was the Americans' main attack or a diversion to draw the British forces from Fort George, Brock left for Queenston, but has his second-in-command, General Sheaffe, and the main British force stay behind at Fort George.

Brock met a messenger along the road who had news that a great number of the enemy had already crossed the river and more were coming. Brock sent the messenger to Fort George to bring General Sheaffe and his troops along as quickly as possible.

Queenston village was situated at the foot of Queenston Heights, a steep cliff rising some 350 feet above the Niagara River. The British had strategically placed a gun at the top of the Heights. The Americans came up behind the British gunners by a steep and narrow path. Taken by surprise, the British beat a hasty retreat.

Understanding the seriousness of the situation, Major-General Brock did not wait for General Sheaffe. Instead, he rallied a small force and charged up the steep hill, sword drawn!

Although he broke the ranks of the American force, he was struck down. The British lines faltered and retreated to the foot of the hill with their fatally wounded leader.

General Sheaffe had just arrived and took command. He ordered his troops to strike inland. Led by Aboriginal guides, Sheaffe managed a surprise attack on the American flank. Although the Americans had a sizeable force that outnumbered their opposition, they panicked and tried to escape. American troops still on their own side of the river were ordered to cross, but refused. Those on the Newark side rowed or swam back, or drowned; the remainder surrendered to the British.

The spring of 1813 saw better-trained American forces at the front, ready to launch yet another major invasion. On May 25th, hundreds of American cannons opened fire on Fort George. The casualties were enormous, and by morning Fort George was just smoldering rubble. The remaining garrison force fled to safety. American forces, under the cover of a morning fog, crossed the river and landed on British soil.

The British retreated to Hamilton and eventually managed to halt the onslaught at Stoney Creek and Forty Mile Creek. The Americans were forced to retire back to Niagara.

American Army engineers quickly refortified Fort George. They even dug up the cemetery of St. Mark's Anglican Church in order to enlarge their fortifications. The poor townspeople of Newark were at the mercy of the invading force, and anyone sympathetic to the enemy was jailed.

By December, British forces had rallied and advanced on Niagara. The Americans abandoned the district and retired across the river. They torched Niagara first, and only two buildings out of one hundred and fifty remained by morning.

The British reoccupied Fort George, and later attacked and captured Fort Niagara on the American side. On December 24th, 1814, the Treaty of Ghent ended the war. The Americans had lost against the British.

In the late 1820s Fort George was abandoned by the military and fell into ruin. The cavalry did stable here during the Rebellion of 1837, however by the time of Confederation, in 1867, the fort was in total disrepair. Locals had even dismantled buildings for firewood, and eventually the military establishment became a farmer's field.

Blockhouses 1, 2, and 3 at Fort George.

During the 1930s the Niagara Parks Commission completely restored Fort George to its former glory. Since 1969, Parks Canada has administered the fort as a national historic site.

Today Fort George is seen by some as an historic destination. Some visitors, however, see more than that. They see the dead who occupied this site prior to and during the War of 1812. A wide range of phenomena haunts the fort, from rapping, knocking, cold spots, and footsteps, to moaning, crying, scents, and strange breezes. Many people experience overwhelming feelings of terror, sorrow, anguish, and nausea. The psychokinetic phenomena includes piano playing, furniture moving, doors opening and shutting, poking, and playing with people's hair. These are simply evidence of far more important phenomena.

Kyle Upton conducts ghost-walk tours of the fort. "I have been running the ghost tours through Fort George since 1994. When I started, I didn't believe in ghosts, but that belief has changed considerably due to my experiences through the years. I have heard things, I have felt things, and I have seen things. Sometimes I have been more surprised than the people I'm guiding and sometimes I am afraid."

By 1999 Kyle had toured 8,000 people through Fort George. That same year he published ghostly accounts in a book titled *Niagara's Ghosts at Fort George.*

The tour begins at the front gates and passes by the sentry box, the cottage, Brocks-Bastion, blockhouse 1 and blockhouse 2, the officers' quarters, the guardhouse, the sawpit, and the woodyard. Straight ahead of the gates are the artificer's building, the officers' quarters kitchen, and the powder magazine. The powder magazine, ironically, is the only original building to survive the War of 1812.

Past the magazine is the tunnel entrance, extending some twenty-two metres (seventy feet) underground and connecting to the octagonal blockhouse. In this tunnel people see shadowy figures and hear footsteps. It is not uncommon for people to flee the tunnel and run for the front gates after an experience.

Heather Baures, of California, visited the Fort on Sunday, June 11, 2000. She told me of her experience. "The tunnel curves, so I was unable to see the tour guide, who had the only light in the dark tunnel. I got the impression that someone was standing behind me. When I turned around, I could see the entrance to the tunnel, which was only a gray rectangle of moonlight. On either side of the tunnel, there were two

The tunnel at Fort George, where visitors report seeing shadows.

men. The one on the right stepped forward and extended his arm toward the other man. After holding it there a moment, he stepped back and dropped his arm to his side. He then knelt down and leaned forward. It looked like he was picking up something. I could tell the men were wearing late-eighteenth-century clothing and the one on the right was wearing a tricorne hat. I believed in ghosts before I went to Fort George; now my beliefs are definitely confirmed."

Barb Cole, of Toronto, has been on the ghost tour three times. On her first tour she and her husband heard many things but nothing actually happened. On the second tour, with her children, something did. "My children and I were visiting the fort in the daytime, after having taken the ghost tour the night before. It was in the afternoon, a time not as busy as the morning that we toured the fort. We had gone through the tunnel and up the lookout. We were the only ones there at that time.

"We came back through the tunnel when my fourteen-year-old son saw a white, shadowy figure on the wall in the back of the tunnel where we had just been. It looked to me like a large spot on the wall, perhaps a patch of daylight, but after a few minutes it formed into the shape of a man. It ran to the other side of the tunnel where it vanished. I could not see facial features but I saw a human shape with arms and legs. It was all white."

Kyle tells of a visitor who fled the fort after her experience. On that visit, as the woman exited from the tunnel, she noticed that the electric lights behind her went out, and she remarked upon this to her friend. He friend didn't know what she was talking about. She thought the lights were on. "She saw three shadowy figures materialize from this 'solid cloud of shadow.' These three male figures, who wore tall hats, (she believed that they were soldiers from the War of 1812) then began moving toward her and the entrance to the tunnel. As they came closer, she turned about and fled from the fort as fast as she could go, dragging her astonished friend."

After a tour is finished, Kyle is left alone in the fort. Usually it's near midnight and he often becomes uncomfortable. "At night the fort can be an intimidating place, even for those of us familiar with it. There are some nights when it even gets to me. The atmosphere of the fort changes from that of a tourist attraction to that of a churchyard. The air thickens to the point of oppressiveness, and a haze settles into the corners of your vision, only to vanish as you turn to confront it."

During one of these nights, Kyle did see something. "As I sped to escape from what had become a less-than-comfortable Fort George, I looked into the lit window of blockhouse 1, only to find its light blocked by the shadowy form that filled the portal. Now, I had seen ghosts before, and I'm not spooked easily, but while other ghostly experiences had been curious sensory phenomena, this one hit me at a purely emotional level. I was filled with such a feeling of terror that I contemplated climbing over the high wooden palisades to escape from the fort, rather than risk walking past that building to the front gate. In all my life, only nightmares have imparted the same incredible sense of fear."

The most haunted blockhouse, and the largest, is number 2. This structure contains the supply depot and barracks, and has a staircase in the middle leading to an upper floor. The spirit of a man inhabits the second floor of the building. On one occasion two guides encountered this phantom walking across the second-floor room. Initially one guide, who was preparing to close the building for the night, caught sight of this gentleman when he was standing at the top of the stairs. Repeated requests that the gentleman follow the guide downstairs failed, so the guide approached the man who continued to move away until he was cornered in the room. At the moment the guide was reaching out to touch the man, his partner arrived at the top of the stairs and spoke to him. The guide turned to answer his friend and explain what was happening. As soon as he did this, the man he had cornered disappeared from sight.

Another time, when they were closing up, they heard the man's footsteps upstairs.

Kyle tells of one intriguing encounter in blockhouse 2 in his book. A woman and her son were visiting the blockhouse. While the woman was conversing with the guide, her seven-year-old wandered about the barracks. Soon he was talking aloud in the back corner of the room. The mother took little notice until it was time to leave. Her son refused to go. The guide, sensing something unusual, asked him who he was talking to. The boy answered "the man." He then described the man as the same height as the guide and wearing the same kind of red military uniform.

He wore the same red coat with long tails, however, it had yellow stripes on the cuffs and collars instead of green stripes like the guide's uniform.

Kyle explained, "Now any good historian knows that the British army colour coded its soldiers. Every regiment of troops had a distinctive colour for the 'facing,' or cuffs and collars, of their uniforms. While historians may be aware of this fact, most seven-year-olds are not. Nor are most seven-year-olds aware of the fact that the 100th Regiment, along with wearing yellow-faced coats, were stationed at Fort George just before the War of 1812."

The boy said the man was very unhappy. The poor fellow had no idea how he had ended up in the barracks, or where all his friends had gone. He was frustrated that no one would talk to him or even look at him. He was also angry with all the people coming and going through his home.

The officers' quarters, facing the parade square in the centre of the fort, is probably the eeriest of all — and not for the faint-hearted.

The officers who once occupied the building lived like gentlemen. In their living quarters they attempted to recreate the high material and social standards they were accustomed to in Great Britain.

Blockhouse 2, where a seven-year-old visitor met the spirit of a soldier from the War of 1812. The soldier told the boy that he was confused — who were all these people (tourists) in his space?

The officers' quarters at Fort George. Notice the appearance of an orb in the photograph. Furniture is often rearranged in this room late at night.

The building is laid out to reflect its original appearance. As you enter the front door a sitting room is located on the right side. The central part of the structure contains the dining area and then a games room and personal quarters. These reflected the background, rank, and interests of the officers.

Dinners were sophisticated affairs, complete with fine silverware and china, serving dishes, and decanters of port and sherry. The officers' kitchen is located at the back of the building. Here staff would prepare elaborate full-course dinners.

When I visited, the female employee who greeted me at the main gate mentioned two areas known to be haunted. The first is the officers' quarters. "I will not go near blockhouse 1 at night, nor the officers' quarters. When you walk by the windows of the quarters you get an eerie feeling, like someone is watching you."

According to some staff and visitors, the mirror hanging in the sitting room contains the ghostly image of a woman. This female spirit is described as having long, slightly curly hair. Although the gilt-framed mirror dates back to the 1790s, it is not an original furnishing of Fort George. No one knows who she is. In recent years, she has been seen

Blockhouse 1.

outside of the mirror. One young child on a tour said she wore a "Cinderella dress" and was brushing her hair with a silver-palm hairbrush.

In 1981 major repairs were made to the officers' quarters, leaving the building with gaping holes for a period of time. Four staff members volunteered to sleep over in the barracks to maintain the security of the site. It was midnight and they had just settled down in their sleeping bags when they heard banging and crashing noises coming from the officers' quarters.

Kyle said, "Rushing outside to see what was the matter, they hurried into the building that they were supposed to be guarding. They had arrived too late; there was no one in sight, but some of the furniture on display in the senior officers' wing had been moved around. The puzzled staff returned the out-of-place objects. They decided to shift their bunk space into the sitting room on the far side of the building. When the noises began anew, the four guardians took only seconds to rush into the senior officers' wing. They arrived in time to see the furniture still in the process of being rearranged, dishes sliding across the wooden tables by themselves, armchairs propelled around the room by unseen hands. Stopped in their tracks, they stared in aghast astonishment for a minute, and then fled, screaming, from the building."

The gift shop, located at the back of the fort, was the site of the kitchen for the hospital building next door. It is now the craftsman's, or artificer's, shop. However, the original building also served as a charnal house where terminally ill patients from the hospital were placed. There they awaited their death in the damp cellar area beneath the kitchen — a place where you could lose sight of your town soul. In fact, many patients did. They remain there, waiting to see the light.

In the only written account of an experience in this building, a couple using the washrooms on the side of the building heard the sound of footsteps above them. The building has no second storey today, but a painting that hangs in blockhouse 1, done by a military surgeon stationed in Niagara before the War of 1812, shows the original building had a second storey.

Many people experience a sense of sadness inside and outside the gift and artificer's shops. One employee who worked in the artificer's shop stated, "This was the site of a sixty-bed hospital. Many visitors experience a sense of pain and illness. Many of the dismembered arms and legs were buried just outside the back of this building." Tourists have reported seeing a man dressed in white standing near the building. Could he have been a surgeon?

No matter where you go inside this fort you are bound to confront spirits, or smell an odd odour, see a reflection in a mirror, watch a table move by unseen hands, see a building that no longer exists, or hear a piano playing in the sitting room or the officers' quarters.

I highly recommend that you join Kyle Upton on a ghost walk sometime. It could change your life, or you could be one of those strangely dressed people who ignore the poor sentry at the gate.

Legg's General Store

~ Birr ~

"I have given this place heart and soul for twenty-five years. Things were in need of change and I followed my spirit.

"I've always been a fan of the Civil War, especially of General McPherson. He was a northerner, but beloved by both armies, and he was killed in battle. I realized that he died too young, his life uncompleted. When you work in the public eye there is both happiness and grief in abundance."

Meet Jack Legg, proprietor of Legg's General Store in Birr, Ontario, near London. A deep and abstract thinker, Jack equates the history of General McPherson to the trials and tribulations of today. He is a sensitive man with a gift for inspiring others, as he is inspired by the story of General McPherson's unfinished life.

Jack's store is a serendipitous adventure, a warehouse of eclectic surprises designed to touch the hearts of anyone and everyone who enters therein. He sells almost everything, including: books, Mexican glassware, toys, candy, giftware, Mennonite furniture, homespun sweaters, flowers, plants, nursery stock, statuary, firewood, candles, incense, food,

Legg's General Store in Birr, Ontario.

and numerous other items. His general store is experiential, not to mention magical. No one leaves empty-handed or empty-headed. Jack's passion is his understanding of the past and he loves to share his philosophy with interested customers.

"He [General McPherson] gives me the strength to do anything. I can battle despair or war. I can handle it; if there is an emergency, I can handle it. There is no heaven or hell, it's how you live that counts, how you honour it. I have no fear of dying. Living is the difficult thing."

Jack's interest in General McPherson and his life is unusual. Has that interest actually drawn the spirit of General McPherson to him, or is there some other reason he has appeared on Jack's property?

A Native American practice is to not mention a person's name once they are deceased, as to speak their name is to call them back. Instead the person is referred to by title, such as "grandmother," "mother," or "daughter." Do Jack's thoughts and conversations about General McPherson call him back and keep him there?

General McPherson first appeared to Jack in 1993. "I saw those riding boots and blue trousers down the alley between two outbuildings. I knew it had to be something. Time in this dimension had no minutes or hours." Jack is convinced it was General McPherson.

Next door to Legg's there used to be a tavern that was frequented by the Donnellys, whose spirits are still active in the district. In *Haunted Ontario 1* I wrote about the night of February 3, 1880, when a group of men arrived at the Donnelly homestead, a few miles away from Birr, and savagely beat several family members to death. The hotel once located next door to Jack's general store was a stage-coach stop and stomping ground for the Donnellys.

Tom Donnelly, the son of James and Johannah, was not always welcome at the hotel. George Swartz, the hotel proprietor, was quoted in the *Huron Expositor*, "One day Thomas Donnelly sat in the bar, somewhat under the influence of liquor, when he carelessly pulled a revolver from his pocket, pointed the muzzle over his shoulder and fired, regardless of the consequences. The bullet passed uncomfortably close to Mr. Swartz's head, burying itself in the wall. Donnelly then fired another shot, with as much nonchalance, which lodged in the ceiling."

On the night of the murders, Tom was stabbed repeatedly with a pitchfork and clubbed outside the Donnelly homestead. His body was eventually dragged back inside the house where his skull was laid open with a shovel.

There are ghosts at their homestead, and perhaps Tom is still hoping for a drink — or maybe revenge. The spirit on the property was not seen until after the hotel came down in 1964. Is that just a coincidence or could the presence be a Donnelly? Or are there two spirits?

Although only visible from the legs down, Jack has no doubt that the spirit is General McPherson. Somehow Jack's journey is interwoven with this Civil War general, born James Birdseye McPherson on November 4, 1828, in Sandusky County, Ohio. McPherson grew up in extreme poverty. It was a storekeeper, like Jack, who helped McPherson secure an appointment to West Point, from which he graduated in 1853 at the head of his class.

Major-General William T. Sherman repeatedly used McPherson's army to outflank strong Confederate defence lines. On July 22, 1864, McPherson attempted to repeat the success when General John B. Hood delivered a surprise counterattack southeast of Atlanta. McPherson decided to ride forward to investigate. To his surprise he encountered a force of Confederates, who shot and killed him as he tried to retreat. At the time of his death General Ulysses S. Grant is reported to have said, "The country has lost one of its best soldiers, and I have lost my best friend."

Coincidentally, Jack's mother's family was from Michigan and lived there at the time of the Civil War. The state of Michigan played an active role during the war against the Confederates, as did London, Ontario, and the district including Birr. Orlo Miller, author of *London*, wrote, "The American Civil War had a deep and lasting effect on the history of Canada, and nowhere was it felt more strongly than in London. The North stood for paid labour, the South for slave labour. The North represented the working man, the South, the Establishment.... The economic picture had changed rapidly. The farmers of the western part of the province of Ontario had greeted the outbreak of the Civil War with some enthusiasm, expecting an increased demand for their wheat." The agricultural development of Kansas soon met that demand, but the Northern armies required beef. Canadian farmers immediately responded by supplying the army with meat. During the Civil War many new farmhouses in the London area were built by beef barons.

The northern armies also required volunteers to fight the South, and many Ontarians who had relatives in the northern states left to join the northern forces. Many never returned.

It was rumoured that gold was hidden somewhere in the hotel next to the general store. Jack said, "Apparently someone back in 1854 had stopped in for a drink and mentioned he was going to buy some land in the area. He even admitted to having the money to buy it. That night he was rolled for his money. However, the stranger's money never surfaced. The culprit had the gold coins in the keg room of the tavern on a ledge. Unfortunately for the thief, the box containing the coins fell behind the ledge and disappeared."

Jack's father, Jack Sr., purchased the property in 1947. Jack took over the business in 1967. Jack Sr. was a very generous man. He operated an extensive business that included dry goods, a lumber mill, and a grist mill. Jack compares his dad's business to an Eaton's store. Whatever people needed you could bet Jack Sr. stocked it. He was also known for his generosity — he fed anyone who arrived on his premises hungry.

In 1964 Jack Sr. decided to demolish the tavern. While removing some floor boards he discovered a box containing six gold coins. The hidden treasure had been found! The discovery of coins had a profound effect on Jack Jr. Today, Jack knows the power of gifting by way of coins.

At his general store, Jack encounters people from all walks of life. He can sense the tragedy that touches many. "I've been a lucky fellow. I collect some of the coins that come into the store and put them on a shelf near the front counter."

Jack offers these coins to bring people good luck. When he meets someone in despair he hands them a coin. "I hope you take this with you." To the amazement of the person, something good usually happens to them. Jack's gift of coins is a gift in many ways.

"A lady once came into the store for some mint chocolates. I said I didn't have any. She then told me about a tragic snowmobile accident that had happened in front of her house. Two young boys were travelling down the road and collided with a vehicle. She felt responsible because it happened in front of her home. I gave her a coin. Then she disappeared.

"Two weeks later a different woman came in the store and thanked me for giving the coin to her son. There were tears in her eyes as she said, 'I want you to meet him.' The son was suffering from a severe head injury. He shook my hand and thanked me for this lucky coin. Apparently he was to have had surgery, but ended up not needing it. I had no idea how this woman obtained the coin. My wife was a witness to all this. Then I began to wonder who the woman was who had come in two weeks earlier worried about a snowmobile accident in front of her home. She had to be an angel. How else would this other woman have received one of my coins?"

There is no question that Legg's General Store is haunted and there is no question that Jack Legg can see and feel more than most. Does his spirit friend inspire some of his insight? Is it a special sensitivity he has, or is his store a place where the separation of a dimension is not so pronounced? The energy there is very different. I feel that the longer I linger the more likely I am to be surprised by a spirit.

"Is a man a lighthouse?" Jack asked me. He asks many odd-seeming questions like that; he expresses himself in images, often jarring and not immediately relevant to the conversation. Who or what is prompting him?

This particular question opened the door for me to understand Jack Legg. "Is a man a lighthouse?" Jack is!

General McPherson was! They shine a light, set an example, gift a coin, ask a surprise question, or make an unusual statement; they are spirits, expressing the moment, one more visible than the other. If I were to be haunted by a spirit, I would certainly choose to have it be an inspirational haunting like the one in Birr. Don't drive on by; stop in for a snack, a gift, a moment of philosophy, and perhaps a sighting.

The Albion Hotel
~ Bayfield ~

The historic village of Bayfield, perched above the sandy shoreline of Lake Huron, has a tradition of civic pride. Folks here are very friendly. During our visit we experienced one of the warmest welcomes my wife and I have ever had anywhere. The Albion Hotel was the warmest welcome of all.

The Albion Hotel is located on Bayfield's main street and it feels just like home. The staff are courteous and welcoming. The structure was built in the 1840s, originally designed to be a store. The proprietor, Robert Reid, built an addition in 1856 and the Albion opened its doors as a hotel. Since that time the hotel has catered to the needs of villagers and tourists.

In 1897 it was the scene of a murder.

The village of Bayfield got its start as a port. Rich agricultural land to the east produced valued crops for shipping and fishing had a lot to offer. Lake Huron is beautiful to start with and here was a spot with a natural harbour and a river mouth, an ideal location for a settlement. The land upon which the village was founded was originally purchased, sight unseen, by Baron van Tuyll van Serooskerken of Hague. He had been advised to do so by his good friend Admiral Henry Bayfield, who served as a surveyor on the Great Lakes. The settlement took the admiral's name.

Bayfield is laid out on a radial plan with a town square at the hub of the wheel. The main street is situated at the northwest corner of one of the spokes. By the 1850s that main street was a hub of activity, with many shops and industry. There were half-a-dozen hotels operating throughout the village and there was an air of abundance.

Unfortunately, it was not to last. The new railway line bypassed Bayfield, built instead at Goderich, just a few miles up the Lake Huron shore. Bayfield's industry withered and died.

Fortunately, the locals were a resourceful lot and soon this picturesque village began to recover. Perhaps the railway did them a favour, because instead of industry they got tourists and an abundance of lovely summer homes.

The local newspaper attested to this in 1895: "A few years ago Bayfield was little heard of outside the country; today she is talked of and widely famed as a pleasant and beautiful watering place."

Tourists fell in love with the quaint atmosphere of the village and its beautiful landscape. The trees there are magnificent; even today there is a slippery elm reported to be 560 years old.

Although serene on the surface, as in any community there were secrets, distrust, alcohol abuse, and even murder. Murder can create a situation in which one or more souls become trapped at the scene of the crime. This, no doubt, explains one aspect of the paranormal activity occurring at the Albion Hotel.

In the 1890s Maria and Edward Elliott were the proprietors of the Albion, and it was also their home. The Elliotts had much sorrow in their family. By 1895 they had already buried three sons; the youngest had been only fourteen years old and the eldest was twenty-eight when they died.

Maria, her daughter Lily, and her two sons, Fred and Harvey, shared the daily chores at the hotel. It was well-known that Harvey had an argumentative nature that became worse when he drank.

On a Monday in November of 1897, twenty-one-year-old Harvey and his friend Dumart went out drinking in nearby Varna, a village located 4 miles (6.4 kilometres) from Bayfield.

At about eight-thirty p.m. Harvey and Dumart returned home to the Albion. It didn't take too long for Harvey to have yet another drink at the bar, now the dining room, and then to quarrel with his nineteen-year-old brother, Fred. There was trouble brewing. The boys left the bar.

Fred was standing outside the hall door. Harvey was standing on the platform in front of the hotel. He shouted to Fred, "Go into the house."

George Erwin, a witness to the events, stated that he heard Harvey swearing at his brother. Harvey was in a temper and Erwin and his sister Lily tried to restrain him from striking his brother. Lily screamed for help.

The family knew that the brothers were not in the habit of quarrelling, except when Harvey had been drinking. Mrs. Elliot rushed to Fred to talk to him. Harvey was only a few feet away when someone caught sight of a revolver in Fred's hand. Fred then shouted, "Keep him away from me or I'll shoot him."

Suddenly Harvey broke away and pulled off his coat. Standing there he yelled, "Here's somebody who is not afraid of being shot."

Then Harvey charged Fred; Fred raised the gun and it went off. Harvey fell into his friend's arms. The bullet had passed through his trachea.

Fred stood still for a moment and then tears welled up in his eyes. He had shot his own brother. Although missing from the newspaper accounts, it was rumoured that they tried to get Harvey to the water pump for a drink before they took him inside.

Harvey was eventually carried into the bar, where he died within seconds. His blood permanently stained the wooden floor.

Fred was tried for murder. The locals took up a petition for clemency but the jury returned a tough verdict: "Guilt; with a strong recommendation to mercy."

The judge sentenced Fred to several years in the Kingston Penitentiary. He was released early due to poor health. He died on September 13, 1905, at the age of twenty-eight.

As for Harvey, it seems he has remained at the place of his death.

Although there have been no visual sightings to confirm the identity, someone likes to turn a light on in the bar area after the hotel has closed for the night. Someone likes to flip a beer tap on occasion, too. Psychics have confirmed a male presence in the new dining room.

Kim Muszynski, the current owner of the Albion, had no idea the hotel was haunted when he purchased it. "I never heard any stories of spirits or haunting until we began some renovation work downstairs."

The renovations involved moving the original bar from the left side, as you enter, to the right side. Kim turned the old bar area into an old-fashioned dining room, furnished with simple antiques. The present-day bar is a very friendly place. Copper-topped tables of all sizes and miscellaneous chairs furnish the area. A gas fireplace is both warm and atmospheric. In former years this room was a gathering place and held a player piano.

During the renovations Kim encountered his first indication of paranormal activity. "We finished the work downstairs and were just getting started upstairs.

"I had hired a painter who said that he didn't paint unless there was music playing. So we provided him with a portable stereo. We had all just started working when the radio went off on its own. This happened three times for no apparent reason."

Kim was not convinced the hotel was haunted — but that soon changed. "One night my partner, John, who was sleeping in the next room upstairs in the hotel came into my room twice. He heard his name being called. He thought I had called him, but I hadn't.

"Then, on the second occasion, just when I was about to drift off to sleep, I felt a hand touch my face. I didn't sleep for the rest of the night."

Nancy was a young woman who married a local farmer by the name of John. The odd thing was that she never went to live with her husband. Instead, she lived at the Albion Hotel, in the room that Kim had used as a bedroom and is now the common room. Her husband visited the hotel to be with her.

Nancy lived there until she died. Perhaps she still calls her husband's name in the night.

There has been activity over the years, particularly during any renovations, but it had been quiet for the last few months. That is, until I made an appointment for an interview.

The night before I arrived, Kim had a very unusual experience at his home. "I have two dogs. When I went to feed them I took a cup of dog food and filled the first dish, then I got a cup for the other one and put that in the dish. What the — the cup was full of water! Where did that water come from? I checked the dogs' pail and it was full of water. It wasn't possible for any water to get in there. I thought it was a prank or something.

"Then at nine a.m. the next morning I was the hotel, sitting in the pub reading your book *Haunted Ontario*, and occasionally glancing up to watch the Olympics on the television. A guest staying in Room 4 came down and inquired if the bar television was connected to the television in his room. I said it wasn't. It's all cable. He said that he was watching CNN when someone or something changed the channel."

When my wife and I arrived at the Albion we were warmly greeted by Kim, Shelly Know, the hotel manager, Jack (Kim's dad), and Stella and Betty, Jack's friends. Jack informed me that Betty is sensitive to spirit activity and wanted to join in the investigation.

The tour of the hotel began in the dining room, which was originally the bar area where Harvey Elliott had died. Kim said the gun Fred used to kill his brother was found behind the bar.

Betty said, "I feel three spots in this room that give me the chills. I have goosebumps on my arms. The presence is male."

Upstairs there are seven bedsitting rooms. Kim led us into the common room, which had been Kim's bedroom. Shelly Know, who has managed the hotel for the past several years, spoke about the unexplained activity in the building. "Not many years ago we were hosting the annual golf tournament. We were sitting in this common room folding T-shirts when four books suddenly flew off the bookcase. The employee with me fled downstairs." Shelly placed the books back on the shelf and went back to the pub. She returned later to discover the same books back on the floor again.

"Another day, after closing, we were sitting here in the common room when we heard the door at the top of the stairs open and close. We were the only ones in the building. Then we heard footsteps."

One night Shelly and three other employees got the shock of their lives in the pub area. "It was midnight and we were closed. There we were sitting on a bench facing the bar. The Rickard's Red tap suddenly turned on all by itself and started spraying beer all over the bar and onto the floor."

During renovations in 2000, Shelly and an employee named Judy shared an experience upstairs. At the time all the doors on the second floor had been removed. The women were sitting in the office, just off the common room. "We heard the door at the top of the stairs open, but there was no door to open! We call this ghost Molly."

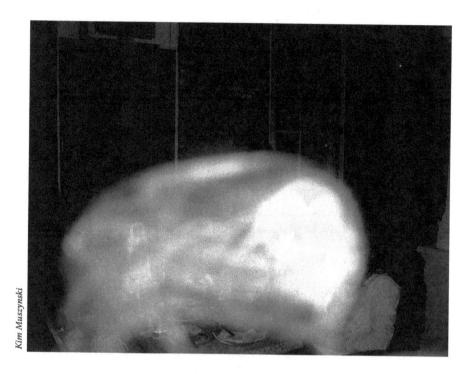

Kim Muszynski

The spirit energy was captured on film outside of the Albion Hotel. Believe it or not there are people seated in this energy having lunch!

Shelly also told me about a light in the dining room alcove that comes on by itself during the night. Betty confirmed that there is activity in that alcove.

One night three weeks before, during the dinner hour, Lisa Muszynski, Kim's sister and one of the chefs, was standing behind the bar when she saw two glasses hanging from a rack move forward and crash to the floor.

Local historian Reg Thompson came to share some information with us as well. Reg is extremely knowledgeable about the history of the area, and has personally researched the murder of Harvey Elliott. Does Reg think the Albion Hotel is haunted?

"I really couldn't say. I haven't seen a glass of beer fly off the shelf, but when it's quiet in the evening and only one or two people are in the pub, sometimes we think someone has just come through the front door. We hear it. The conversation stops. No one comes in to the bar and no one goes out either. You never hear anything else."

Kim has a suggestion to make if you want to book a specific room: "I had a couple staying in Room four. It was late at night. I only had one room booked. At twelve-thirty a.m. we closed the hotel and left for the night. The next morning our guests came down and asked who was playing the guitar downstairs the previous night. They were surprised there was no applause after the playing ended. I checked with all the employees, but there had been no one in the building at the time.

"A group of friends and I decided to go down the street after closing time. One of the girls in the group was not feeling well. She decided to retire to Room 4 until we returned. We got back at two-thirty a.m. The poor girl was terrified. She had heard footsteps going back and forth and back and forth in the hallway. She knew she was the only person in the building."

Mike Parkinson, a chef, had an amazing experience one New Year's Eve. Mike and Lisa were upstairs after dinner, readying themselves for the New Year's festivities. "After we did dinner we went up and showered and changed. We were about to come downstairs to join the party. The time was eleven-forty-five p.m. I came out of the room. I opened the door to go downstairs. I saw a figure sitting on the last two steps facing the front door. No one else was in the area. The woman appeared bulky around the shoulder area. Her head was bent down. I let go of the door to get Lisa and then I thought 'who was that?'

"I opened the door again, but she was gone. People were now milling around the front hallway. I looked for her in the crowd but she was nowhere to be seen. Then on New Year's Day I was there at the hotel doing the inventory. I know I was not alone in the building."

An interesting cast of characters is in this little village, ghosts and otherwise. It is a gorgeous setting and has a wonderful welcome mat. Should you miss this stop? Not a ghost of a chance!

Avon Theatre

~ Stratford ~

The lights go down; the curtain goes up. A solitary figure stands in the shadows. The silence is all-encompassing.

Do the dead walk among us? Take heed, for they thirst for the souls of the living. And you are here with them. Welcome to the haunted Avon Theatre.

A woman sits in her balcony seat. Her gaze is focused on the actors and actresses on stage. For a brief moment her eye catches the gentleman seated next to her. His face is pale and stone cold. She wonders if he is ill. He turns his head, stares blankly, and then slowly vanishes before her eyes. She faints.

There is a phantom in the Avon Theatre in Stratford, Ontario. Could it be the eccentric janitor who once lived in the building, or perhaps the theatre owner Ambrose Small, who mysteriously disappeared and was never found? Maybe it is an actor who once graced the stage here. It is a mystery.

The Avon Theatre, a familiar downtown Stratford landmark, first opened in 1901 as the Theatre Albert, a well-appointed vaudeville house.

The Theatre Albert was the city's first privately owned legitimate theatre. Prior to 1901, the theatre in the Stratford City Hall was used for such purposes. Fire struck the city hall in 1897, burning it to the ground. Albert Brandenburger, an ambitious entrepreneur who had been bringing theatrical troupes to Stratford for several years, took the opportunity to build his own opera house.

Originally the building had a colonial facade with three front entrances and two small stores at each corner. The front was decorated with four terracotta pilasters, a galvanized iron cornice, and a small balcony over the main entrance.

The Theatre Albert opened with *A Female Drummer*, featuring Nellie O'Neill and Willis P. Sweatman. The theatre soon became a major entertainment centre and a regular location for many touring productions. Over the years it progressed through a series of names and owners. In May, 1910, it was the Griffin Theatre, in 1924 the Majestic Theatre, in 1929 it became a movie house, and in 1937 it became the Avon Theatre under the ownership of Sarnia Theatre Ltd. Finally the Stratford Festival rented it in 1956 and purchased it in 1963.

The haunting of the Avon extends as far back as the early 1920s. Superstition in the theatre is rampant, but sometimes with good reason. Some actors and actresses feel that a full dress rehearsal allows all mistakes to come out prior to opening night; some hang good-luck charms around their mirrors in the dressing room. "Break a leg" is a common expression heard in the wings. Invisible forces of bad luck are thereby acknowledged.

John is a retired stagehand who worked in the Avon Theatre from 1953 until he retired in 1996. He has seen many people come and go over the years. Theatre is almost a heritage for him. His father, Fred, worked in this theatre as a stagehand and a projectionist from 1926 to 1942 and John's son is currently employed there. These generations of theatre employees have enough stories to fill a book. John knows about a spirit who watches performances from the balcony and another, or perhaps the same one, who endlessly walks the building.

There could be more than one spirit. It could be Ambrose Small, who owned the theatre in the early 1900s and disappeared during that time. It could be an old janitor who lived in the alcove off stage left. He never left the building. He was an odd man who liked to tip the bottle. He also disappeared and was never seen again. It seems strange that two people connected to the theatre disappeared and were never found, nor was either mystery solved. Were they murdered? Is there yet another spirit to be found at the Avon Theatre?

Ambrose J. Small was a theatrical entrepreneur who was stage-struck most of his life. His dream was to be a producer. He did produce one play, but it flopped. Instead, he purchased series of theatrical houses across Ontario. Small's flagship theatre was the old Grand Opera House located at the corner of Richmond and King Streets in London, Ontario. Small became wealthy and famous; undoubtedly others were envious.

On December 3, 1919, Small made a million-dollar sale. He took the cheque to the bank and then his wife out to lunch to celebrate. He returned to the Globe Theatre in Toronto and worked part of the afternoon. He left, ostensibly to buy a newspaper, and was never seen again.

John remembers something his mother told him many years ago: "My mother told me that Ambrose Small had made an enemy of a theatre manager." Did an enraged theatre manager do him in? Was Ambrose Small murdered in this theatre? Certainly someone still enjoys sitting in the balcony with the "ladies," watching plays to their heart's content.

Avon employees will admit to feeling a presence. One theatre employee who worked the midnight shift heard noises every night, and confessed to feeling watched and constantly on edge.

John also said, "On one occasion I was working in the left alcove off the stage. I could hear footsteps around me and above me. At the time there were only two or three of us working in the building. I thought my friends were playing a trick on me. I went up to the attic, thinking that this was where the noise was coming from and that my friends would be there. No one was there. The footsteps were very audible. This is a common experience."

Props and tools go missing in this theatre. They are seldom, if ever, found. Perhaps the old janitor is still cleaning up; perhaps there's a play going on simultaneously in another dimension that needs props!

The lights go up. The curtain goes down. The audience goes home, but the figure in the shadow remains.

Mylar and Loreta's

~ Singhampton ~

A woman stands at the entranceway, beckoning you to come forward. Her greeting reminds you of something long forgotten. The furnishings in the room nudge a memory, a savory secret. You are seated at a table with a flickering candle; a menu appears in your hand; your first glance yields the Legend of Mylar and Loreta:

T'was 100 years ago or so that Mylar left his home
To find his fame and fortune, in the new land he would roam
His journey was a long one. But finally he found
A home here in Singhampton, with good friends all around

He talked of a fair lady, the finest in his land
And when the time was ready, he wrote home for her hand
Loreta's heart was bursting, her stately ship set sail
The sky was bright, the sea was calm, no thought of stormy gale

Then came that night of terror when her ship went down at sea
Her soul released to Heaven, her spirit was set free

Some say she came to Mylar, it is difficult to know
His love for her kept growing. He could never let her go

Now as you sit and dine today and enjoy our country inn
Feel the power of their special love that lingers from within

Could this tale be true? If you're a ghost hunter your heart skips a beat at this point. If your curiosity compels you to question, you will discover that a spirit has actually taken up residence here among the living, in the stylish old hotel now converted to a restaurant and pub.

A ghost was discovered at the inn and to explain its existence the tale of Mylar and Loreta was invented. The employees call their resident ghost Mylar, in keeping with the story, and now fact and fiction have become entwined.

The main street of historic Singhampton is the locale of this period hotel from the 1860s. The town, which is located in the township of Osprey in the eastern part of Grey County on the 400-metre- (1,200-foot-) high plateau of the Blue Mountains, dates back to the 1840s when Josiah R. Sing arrived.

Mylar has become somewhat of a celebrity. The ghost sign outside welcomes you to come in and dine, and meet Mylar.

Settlement was slow, the climate unpredictable. Growth came from mills on the local Mad River and the community actually once bore the name "Mad River Mills." Eventually named after its founder, Josiah Sing, Singhampton literally translates to Sing's Town.

The local lumbermen required housing, and hotels filled the bill. Singhampton actually had two hotels located side by side on the main street. The first brick tavern in Singhampton was built in the early 1850s. The business provided accommodation for travellers, land speculators, and survey crews. A second hotel, now Mylar and Loreta's, was constructed sometime in the late 1850s.

The first hotel was called the Lower Hotel. John Stinson owned and operated it until 1865, when it was renamed Stinson's Tavern. Sometime later the name changed to Victoria Inn. It provided housing for horses as well as people, and served meals and liquid refreshments from 10:00 a.m. to 3:00 p.m., primarily to hungry lumbermen. The Upper Hotel, as the other one was known, had a great series of names: the Royal Hotel, the Blackstock Hotel, the Exchange Hotel, the Hampton House, and, ultimately, Mylar and Loreta's.

By 1919, fishermen had discovered Singhampton. They arrived from Toronto by train to fish in the trout-filled streams and rivers. They came for a weekend, a week, or maybe took a room for a month. Singhampton was a tourist mecca. In the 1930s the first May weekend brought more than thirty men to each hotel.

In 1984 Sandy Spencer purchased the Hampton Hotel. Fate played a hand — a kick in the backside makes all the difference in the world. Sandy, an energetic and self-motivated woman, had been living in Collingwood, where she worked as a manager in a busy restaurant. "Why not own your own business if you're going to work so hard?" she thought one day. Sandy was raising two young children and had recently lost her mother. There was a void in her life. She knew she needed a focus.

Her fate brought her to the auction sale of the Hampton Hotel. Could she really afford it? Was this what she was truly meant to do?

On the morning of the auction, Sandy decided to sleep in — the auction momentarily forgotten. Not to be! Sandy was startled from her sleep by a kick to the backside. *Who kicked me?* she thought. No one was there. She noticed the time and decided to get up and attend the auction with her three-year-old son. Sandy will never forget that day! The auctioneer cried, "Do I hear a bid?" Lo and behold, her young son raised his hand. Her son was, of course, not registered, so she was given the opportunity to decline the bid. But that was it. Sandy honoured the bid. She now owned The Hampton Hotel. She had no idea, however, that the place was haunted!

Anne is a kind, middle-aged woman who also finds her fate connected to the old hotel. She has worked in the building for nineteen years. Anne and Sandy had never met until Sandy purchased the property. On the same morning when Sandy was kicked in bed by a spirit, Anne also experienced something unusual. "The morning Sandy was kicked I was sound asleep in bed. I remember waking up when someone or something kicked me in the back. I didn't even know who Sandy Spencer was."

Sandy said, "My mother had recently passed away. I believe it was my mother who kicked me in bed, trying to tell me to get up and go to the auction." Was it?

Did Sandy's mother have her eye on Anne as well? Sandy was going to need help with her new undertaking and her mother must have been aware of that fact. Sandy met Anne and hired her. It was Anne who told her about the spirit who appears in certain places in the building. But Sandy soon had an encounter of her own. "One day I was cleaning the tables in the dining-room area. I looked up and there was a man looking at me. Then he disappeared. He was tall and slender and he wore a red plaid shirt and denim overalls. It looked like he was wearing a straw hat. He appeared to be middle-aged. He was standing right in front of the kitchen doors, just by the dining room entrance."

As you enter the front door of the establishment you walk a short distance before reaching the main entrance to the restaurant. Straight ahead are the kitchen doors. To your left is a spacious dining room. To your right is a quaint, cozy bar with an opening behind for wait staff to place orders to the kitchen. Wooden stools line the bar. The furnishings are old and eclectic and reflect the many periods that this place has known.

One night, at about 10:30 p.m., when Sandy was alone in the restaurant, Mylar appeared. "I was busy behind the bar when I saw him peering at me through the small opening to the kitchen. I thought for a moment 'Who is this guy?' Then he vanished. I went to look, but no one was there. I can never make out his face.

Mylar has been seen standing in the dining room on numerous occasions.

"Another time a customer in the hallway saw a man standing at the sideboard located on the right-hand side. The man was pulling out a drawer. That was one customer I lost. She swore he closed the drawer before he disappeared. I have no idea what he was looking for."

One day the cook and another employee saw a man in a red plaid shirt standing at the back door. They asked him if they could help him and he disappeared in front of them. On another occasion "our cook was cleaning up after the restaurant had closed. There were no customers in the building. She looked out the kitchen doors and saw Mylar sitting at the far end of the bar on a stool. Then he disappeared."

Mylar seems to be fond of table settings. Cutlery in the dining area is moved so often that the staff started to keep watch on the room. Place settings are often reversed. Kitchen items also go missing. Sandy mused, "Too bad he doesn't clean!"

Sandy feels the spirit is lost on this plane, an earthbound soul. She has often talked to him about finding the light. No one knows who he is. Sandy has a feeling or intuitive hunch he was a frequent visitor to the hotel in the 1920s and 30s. One thing is certain: Mylar relates to Anne. He has appeared to her on numerous occasions over the last nineteen

Mylar likes to poke around the kitchen and storage room.

years. He even called to her once: "I was in the dining room and I heard my name called. It was a male voice. No one was there."

Still, Sandy does not feel threatened by the presence. "I believe he is a friendly soul. I have never been frightened of him. He looks like a farmer. He stands about six feet, two inches tall and has a slim build.

"Last fall a traveller stopped in for something to eat. She told me she was a healer. As soon as she stepped in the door she said there is a spirit here, a man. She had dinner and left."

95

Mylar has been seen seated at the bar, on the stool to the far right. Perhaps he is waiting for a drink.

Spirits are often attracted to individuals who are "sensitive." When Anne was asked if she had ever had any early experiences with spirits she nodded. "When I was nine years old I lived in Simcoe. I remember I was in my bedroom and curled up in bed with a magazine. Suddenly the pages started to turn on their own. That was strange, and yet it didn't really frighten me. I realized it might have been the young girl who died in a fire in the basement before we owned the house."

Anne paused a moment and recalled another experience with her mother. "I was living in Delhi in a Victorian farmhouse with my parents. I was always terrified of staying alone in that place. My mother often said an older man, a spirit, would be seen walking through the house and the attic. She once told me he had spoken to her. He said, 'Tell your daughter not to be afraid. I am looking after her.'" Perhaps he is still looking after her. Maybe he even kicked her in bed!

When asked why she has worked so long in one place, she replies, "This is my extended family." She is, of course, including Mylar.

Mylar is seen at the back door of the kitchen and at the entranceway of the dining room. Although he is held responsible for moving cutlery in the restaurant, he has never been seen in the room. Mylar seems to like to sit at the bar and also to poke his head through the kitchen opening. Seems he's quite at home, opening drawers and moving things about, looking for God knows what.

Overalls, plaid shirt, straw hat, Mylar could have been a local farmer waiting for his beloved to arrive.

One thing you can count on at Mylar and Loreta's, you'll never have to dine alone.

Gravenhurst Opera House

~ Gravenhurst ~

Throughout Muskoka many spirits have lingered, to paint, to dance, to act, to canoe along the windswept shoreline. One can sense the magic that permeates Muskoka, a land that has cast its own spell and haunted young and old alike. Here artisans have enjoyed the beauty of nature and water for a century and a half. Many souls refuse to leave only their memories behind.

The first tourists came in 1860 by boat to Washago, and then by stage or foot to McCabe's Landing in Gravenhurst. Alexander Cockburn made Gravenhurst a lake port when he launched the *Wenonah* in 1866, the first, but not the last, steamer on Lake Muskoka.

The Northern Railway was extended to Gravenhurst in 1875. It was a twelve- to fourteen-hour trip from Toronto. A spur line was laid to McCabe's Landing, where trains were met by the Cockburn company steamers. Tourists could then continue on to Bala or Port Carling. In those days the cottagers stayed all summer.

In 1887, with a population of 2,200, Gravenhurst officially became a town. Shortly after its incorporation, fire destroyed the entire business district. Although the town promptly rallied to rebuild, fire struck again in 1897 and the town hall burned down. By 1901 the magnificent Gravenhurst Town Hall and Opera House was built.

On opening night, the *Gravenhurst Banner* printed this account,

> The music, songs, choruses and dancing were of the highest standard and most heartily enjoyed by the audience; the whole affair being a huge success. The sale of tickets commenced last Friday at the corner drug store. Considerable interest was at once manifested and, by the time of the show, every reserved seat had been taken. There were 152 seats at 50 cents, 130 seats at 35 cents, and 130 seats at 25 cents. The proceeds of the concert, almost $150, are to be used for stage decorations and the future installation of opera chairs.

In 1934, the Gravenhurst Opera House established the first summer theatre in Canada, thanks to Toronto radio performers John Holden, Isabel Palmer, and Babs Hitchmann. They were known as the Good Companions. The *Banner* wrote, "Will Gravenhurst support worthwhile shoes? The capacity audience that greeted John Holden and his Good Companions at the Opera House tonight amply demonstrated the answer. The whole company made a decided hit in Gravenhurst."

Canadian-born Holden studied drama in the United States. May Robson, the actress, encouraged Holden to join the Bonstelle Players of Detroit. Holden performed as an actor for four years, touring small towns and also working on Broadway. When his father died in 1929, Holden returned to Toronto. He ventured into radio and rose to prominence while working at CFRB. He quickly became a household name when he accompanied Foster Hewitt on his early General Motors' hockey broadcasts.

The Straw Hat Players, a company of outstanding Canadian actors and actresses from all parts of the country, first performed in Gravenhurst on July 21, 1948. One member of this fine troupe was Barbara Hamilton. From 1948 through 1955, the Straw Hat Players performed sixty-two different productions at the Gravenhurst Opera House, a total of three hundred and eight performances.

Eventually, town officials in Gravenhurst decided to pull up roots and move the town government elsewhere. Gravenhurst researcher J.P. Stratford describes the fate of the opera house: "Although abandoned by politicians, the now label-confused building remained managed and funded by elected officials as a community property."

A committee was quickly spearheaded by Gordon Sloan to rejuvenate the opera house. A plan was conceived for upgrading the neglected building. Between 1969 and 1972, $200,000 was spent refurbishing the opera house. On September 26, 1972, the opera house officially reopened featuring the premiere performance of *Guys and Dolls*.

On February 23, 1993, Gravenhurst experienced its darkest day when Ministry of Labour officials padlocked the front doors of the opera house for safety reasons. An accelerated moisture problem was causing structural damage to parts of the building. There were concerns that the building might collapse under a winter snow load. An estimated $3,000,000 would be needed to restore the structure. Town officials and caring citizens lobbied the government for financial aid, along with their own fundraising activities. To everyone's amazement their efforts proved successful. On February 4, 1995, the Gravenhurst Opera House reopened after a classy facelift.

In 1997, the town officials went in search of a town arts and culture manager. They found Ross A.J. Carlin, an entrepreneur and recipient of the Governor General's Award. He created a mission statement for this cultural centre and a high-profile image for the opera house, which today represents the very best of what Gravenhurst means to its citizens.

Ross was the first person I spoke to about supernatural activity at the opera house. I asked him if he thought the place was haunted. "Absolutely! I would think that over one hundred years of events have given many credible people experiences that are unexplained." Completely believable but unexplained happenings include sudden door openings, mysterious footsteps, lights turning on and off, and being touched by an invisible hand.

"The apparition would eventually be named Ben. Anything and everything to go wrong at the Opera House would eventually become attributed to Ben's ghostly presence," reported the *Banner* newspaper.

Ross feels the spirits are attracted to the energy. "The nature of the building, with so much raw emotional experience, could draw a spirit to it. If I was a spirit I would like to live here."

Although he personally has never seen an apparition, he has certainly had a haunted experience. "In January 2000, I was working late on a Friday night. I was all alone in the building. When I was ready to leave, I shut my computer off, closed my office door and locked it. I then turned out the lights and locked the front doors as I left the building.

"I was the first person in the opera house the following morning. The time was about eight a.m. There was no sign that anyone had entered since I had left the night before. I went to my office and unlocked the door. As I entered, I turned on my computer. When I bent over to turn on the printer I noticed a piece of paper had been printed during my absence. One line had been typed on the page. It read: 'what's happening to me?' I turned off the computer and the lights and went home!"

Ross also recalled another unexplained experience he had while working in the opera house. "It was the same month as the computer incident. I was in the process of interviewing a young woman for a job. I took her upstairs to tour the theatre. As we were walking down the aisle toward the stage, I remarked to her that we had a resident ghost. At that moment the chandelier hanging over the stage went on and off several times, right on cue! At the time there was no power turned on in the theatre. I guess that was the spirit's way of saying hello!"

Shortly thereafter, during the Gravenhurst Winter Carnival festivities, American clairvoyant Mary Ellen Rodriguez was asked to try to communicate with the spirits of the opera house. Ms. Rodriguez was successful. The *Banner* newspaper published her results: "Although claiming to identify the presence of numerous transient spirits from the past, the only spirit resident, she said, was an invisible theatre worker, an actor, beside her on the stage, named John."

Subsequent debate has prompted speculation that the spirit John may, in fact, be the incarnation of Muskoka summer theatre founder John Holden. According to the *Banner*, "The first report of an apparition surfaced around 1960. It was identified as one of the building's construction crew from 1900–01. Apparently distraught following rejection by a young local actress, the Town Hall workman was said to have fallen to his death from the bell tower during construction. The emergence of the unnamed man's ghost was believed to be his unrequited spirit awaiting his true love's stage entrance, an event that would never happen."

Lee Madden has worked as a volunteer at the opera house during the reconstruction phase and afterward. One day, while working alone, she had an experience. "I was alone in the building when I suddenly heard someone running below in the back of the building on the first floor. Then a door slammed. The doors in the opera house are not designed to slam. The door hinges prevent this from happening. I went downstairs to check but no one was in the building. I returned upstairs."

Lee could never have imagined what happened next. "I felt a cold draft on my back. Then I felt a hand on my shoulder. I turned around but nothing was there. We had often talked about a ghost in the building. We called him Benny, and always blamed him when things went missing. I said, 'Benny, leave me alone. I'm trying to get some work done.' I didn't feel scared."

My third interview was with Dona Rolston, whose office was located in the opera house. "I believe there is only one spirit in the opera house," he told me. "There has been a great deal of speculation as to who the spirit is. I felt the presence was masculine. The sounds made were like someone working with their hands. You could hear the noise of a hammer banging. All the sounds were associated with construction work.

"I also had patrons complain on numerous occasions about cold areas in the building, as though someone was blowing cold air on their shoulders. I heard actors say that they would never get dressed alone in the opera house. You could always feel a cold breeze coming down the stairs from the second floor."

Early one Saturday morning, Dona encountered the presence of a spirit on the second floor. "At nine a.m. I arrived at the opera house. I opened the front door and proceeded to my office, located behind the stage. As I entered the office I heard a horrendous crash, like an aluminum ladder falling. I ran out onto the stage. There was nothing there. I thought it was Len, who was the maintenance worker. I called out his name. No one answered.

"I went back to my office and sat down at my desk. I started working but I felt that something was not quite right. It was then that I noticed that someone had turned off my radio.

"Fifteen minutes later, I heard the crash again. I went back out, and this time I checked the whole building. I was all alone and the opera-house doors were locked. Regardless, I could really feel the presence of someone around me. I returned upstairs and walked out on stage. I said, 'Okay, you obviously don't want me to be here today. Give me a few minutes and I'll be leaving.'"

In July 2000, the Follows family arrived in Gravenhurst to star in a one-month production of *Hay Fever*. They experienced a series of happenings in the opera house that summer. The Follows family know the opera house. Ted Follows was one of the original Straw Hat Players and first acted in the Gravenhurst Opera House in 1952.

According to Laurence Follows, actor and producer of such plays as *Forever Plaid*, *Stomp*, and *Forever Tango*, the Gravenhurst Opera House is indeed haunted. "During the summer I had heard about the ghost stories. People would joke about them. I hadn't really thought about it or paid any attention to the stories until something happened one night. I was backstage during the third act of the play. It was dark outside by this time. I was near the back stairway when something came around the corner. Then this shadow went down the stairs. I followed it, but there was nothing there." This was a whole new experience for Laurence at the opera house. What was that shadow?

More things happened to Laurence during the month of July. He heard unexplained bumps and bangs. The energy in the building seemed heavy. Laurence invited two friends from Toronto, Valerie Farquharson and Leslie Krumins, to come to the opera house in the hope that they could explain what was going on.

"They toured the basement. One original exposed wall still remains in that part of the building. Valerie walked over and placed her hand on the wall. She started picking up information. She actually tuned into some of the previous council meetings that had occurred here and she sensed trouble.

"She said she opened up a channel and then started closing doorways to allow the trapped energy to flow out. My God, it changed the whole space. A new lightness of energy could be felt on stage."

Valerie had a number of experiences. "There was this entity that would come and go. I also encountered a portal — a doorway or vortex of energy. There were ghosts of theatre people who had been involved in stage productions over the years. I sensed the presence of the builder of the opera house and the young architect who designed it."

One entity had concerns about the original inspiration for the opera house. Valerie explained, "The dream was to inspire people to come together. The spirit did not want to ever see the opera house close. Yet, the spirit was troubled. It was unable to communicate with the living. It was frustrated at not being heard. Each time the spirit attempted to communicate, the spectator would flee. Sometimes as human beings we can mirror our own fears."

I asked Valerie who the spirit was. She replied "John Holden. I can also see a woman near him. She is not always with him. He brings other people in."

When Valerie and Leslie returned they encountered other spirits who wished to communicate. "We came together on another visit with John Holden and many others … some had been connected directly with him during his time and various others had been connected with the opera house from its original conception and building, and some of them over the hundred years of its existence.

"The group was like a large council of sorts with John as a major spokesperson. This was important for many of them because of the hundredth anniversary of the opera house and the beginning of a new millennium. They had to find a person or persons who would communicate with them in order to help clear old karma and to assist in creating a new portal for the past to leave through and the new transformation to enter in.

"What occurred during the six to eight weeks of the summer of 2001 at the opera house was the beginning of a very positive 'environmental' shift."

No doubt a whole cast of actors and actresses, seen and unseen, will come and go at the Gravenhurst Opera House. No matter what world they belong to, this real world or the world of enchanted Muskoka, you should take it in. When the curtain rises, we might all see something different. The stage is set.

Calhoun Lodge
~ Massasauga Provincial Park ~

As the sun sinks low on the horizon of Blackstone Harbour, surprised paddlers raise their eyebrows when they hear the sweet strains of a country violin.

Sitting by the campfire in the Massasauga Provincial Park, south of Parry Sound, stories of the haunting of Calhoun Lodge are recounted. Some folks refuse to paddle near the lodge. Other campers deliberately approach the lodge at night to catch a glimpse of a ghostly figure, or to hear footsteps approaching on the moist moss-covered rocks that surround the dwellings. Does someone walk here still and serenade the sunset?

Calhoun Lodge at Blackstone Harbour, near the Moon River, once had a caretaker. He was quite a character, Jerome Cascanette. Most evenings he fancied a drink and a puff of tobacco while he played his fiddle. On a still summer eve his high-pitched chords wafted across the water. He had a history. He was more or less a loner, a man who had fought for his country in the Second World War as a machine gunner, a man who had witnessed the death of many comrades-at-arms. The carnage of war had changed him. He was a different man. The cries of his comrades who had fallen in battle

The old log cabin served as shelter prior to the construction of Calhoun Lodge in the 1930s.

echoed in his ears. He turned his attention to trapping, guiding, boat-building, and fiddle playing. Jerome lived a solitary existence in a cabin on Conger (Pine) Lake before he went to work at Calhoun Lodge.

During the 1920s, Joseph Calhoun, a successful lawyer from Cleveland, Ohio, discovered the pristine landscape of Blackstone Harbour. It was here he chose to hunt and fish with his American friends in the spring and in the fall. For many years Joseph or "Judge" Calhoun, as he was often dubbed, was content to camp on his excursions. In 1939 he was presented with the opportunity to purchase the 300 acres where he loved to camp. Local residents, including Jerome's father, William Cascanette, and his uncle, were hired to build a main lodge on the property. Local materials were used and a long-time friend by the name of George Washington Brown built the stone chimney. Front and side porches were added later, and a kitchen building was connected to the main lodge by two doors. The Judge was an imposing man, strong and broad, standing six feet, four inches tall. He had a passion for gardening and several flower beds adorned the property.

Massasauga Provincial Park

Judge Calhoun, still a great outdoorsman in his later years, paddling his canoe to a favourite fishing spot.

Massasauga Provincial Park

Joseph Calhoun poses for a picture before heading out on a hunt.

The Calhoun's named their estate Willebejobe, derived from the first names of the family: William, Betty Jo, and Betty.

Hospitality was vital to the Judge and his sensitivity and caring attitude involved him with the local people. He often gave away his vegetables, and even the odd chicken, to someone in need of food. The door of Calhoun Lodge was always open to anyone who was in need of help, or who wanted to stop in for a cool glass of lemonade while fishing.

In 1963 the Judge needed a new caretaker for the lodge and Jerome Cascanette seemed to be the right choice. Jerome was a thin, wiry man of average height. He settled into the caretakers' house. His duties consisted of grounds maintenance and any odd jobs that need to be done. In the off-season, Jerome lived at the lodge alone, occasionally returning to his cabin to oversee his trapline.

Loneliness sometimes leads to despair. Jerome was in love with a woman from nearby Woods Bay. His passion was, sadly, unrequited. She chose another man to marry and Jerome lost interest in life.

A local resident often delivered mail and food to Jerome at Calhoun Lodge during the winter months. On one occasion a large package was delivered. When Jerome opened the parcel the resident was surprised to see that it was a dress. Apparently, Jerome thought he was going to get the woman, not just the dress, from the Simpsons Catalogue!

By the spring of 1968, Jerome was in poor emotional and mental health. He was often heard conversing with his war buddies who had never returned home from the front. He was only fifty-five years old, but already he was a forgotten and forsaken man.

On the morning of Saturday May 25th, 1968, he rose early. From his closet he selected his Sunday suit, removed it from the hanger, and laid his clothes out on the bed. From there he walked out of the room, down the stairs to the front door, and took the short walk to the water's edge. He washed there and then returned to the house where he dressed in his best.

Then he did something totally out of character and very unorthodox: he broke into the Judge's liquor chest and removed a fine bottle of scotch.

Sometime later Jerome left the lodge carrying the scotch and entered the maintenance shed, located between the lodge and his residence. The bottle was set down on the work bench and his attention turned to the tractor. He had a plan. He started up the tractor and closed the shed door, probably sipped a little more scotch and then lay down on the bench and shut his eyes for the last time.

Jerome's body was discovered the next day by the Judge, who had just arrived for the season. The Judge knew something was wrong when Jerome failed to meet him at the dock; Jerome was always there to greet him! When he entered the lodge, the Judge noticed that the liquor chest had been broken into. Something was very wrong. Not long after, the Judge found Jerome in the maintenance shed, dead.

The *Parry Sound Star* published a brief account in the paper on May 30, 1968:

> Jerome Cascanette, 55, caretaker for many years on the Moon River property, was found dead on May 25th on property owned by Mr. J. Calhoun of Cleveland, Ohio. The property is located on Blackstone Harbour.
>
> Cpl. Campbell and Police Constable Robinson of Parry Sound Ontario Provincial Police investigated the death. Foul play is not suspected.

The Judge sold Calhoun Lodge in 1972. No one in the family was interested in keeping the property. Joseph Calhoun died later that same year. The Taylor family purchased Calhoun Lodge, but sold it in 1974 to the Ministry of Natural Resources. The ministry bought the land during the land assembly for a provincial park, tentatively to be named Blackstone Harbour Massasauga Wildlands Provincial Park. The buildings remained idle until 1990, when park staff began to work in the area. Restoration work and a general clean up of Calhoun Lodge were the cooperative efforts of Employment and Immigration Canada, the Parry Sound Nature Club, and the Ministry of Natural Resources.

In 1993 the provincial park opened for business under the name the Massasauga Provincial Park. This park extends along the east shore of Georgian Bay just south of Parry Sound to the mouth of the Moon River. Massasauga measures almost twenty-one kilometres (thirteen miles) from north to south, and just over twelve kilometres (seven and a half miles) from east to west at its widest point. At 12,810 hectares, the park provides important water access to Georgian Bay and the 30,000 islands, as well as several adjoining inland lakes.

In the summer of 1993, eighteen-year-old Scott Thomas was employed as the first tour guide and caretaker of Calhoun Lodge. Coincidentally, his nickname was Jerome, but he had never heard the story of Calhoun Lodge. Scott fell in love with the natural beauty of the park. To him his job seemed like a calling. He felt he was meant to work there, and as of this writing still does.

In late June of that year, Scott was scraping paint off the old generator shed. Little did he know what was in store for him. "I was the only person on the property at the time. It was late in the day. I was expecting the staff who were out working on the bay to come back for me. Suddenly I heard footsteps on the nearby moss that covered much of the grounds. I could hear the water squishing out of the moss with each footstep. I knew there was someone behind me. I had decided to turn about quickly before my fellow employees could scare me. I turned and my heart went up in my throat. No one was there."

That night Scott and ten other park employees settled in for the night. They were staying in the caretaker's house. Jerome, of course, was the last person to occupy this abode. "The girls slept downstairs and the fellows upstairs. That night the girls heard the tinkling of glass. The sound was keeping time.

"Later the next day, Chantel, one of the park employees, and I were leaving the main lodge building and walking toward the caretaker's house, when I saw something. I saw a figure standing on the screened-in porch. As we approached the building it disappeared into thin air. It looked like a shadow with a head. I could see right through it. It happened so fast. Chantel had been looking down at her feet to watch where she was going and didn't see the shadow. I thought I was crazy. I still didn't know anything about Jerome."

That night at dinner Scott and the girls shared their experiences of the day. Their boss told the group about Jerome and how he had committed suicide in the maintenance shed. The dinner conversation died then, too. Scott set a goal for himself and the park, to research the history of Calhoun Lodge and Jerome Cascanette.

What Scott had not suspected was Jerome's need to connect with him. One day late in the summer of 1993 Scott and another park employee,

Massasauga Provincial Park

Calhoun Lodge, where Jerome Cascanette has remained in spirit since his untimely death.

Anthony, were working in the maintenance shed. Scott was up in the rafters and Anthony was handing him the boards they were to store. The lads worked away with the radio playing in the background.

Scott explains, "We heard the two-way radio go off. Anthony rushed out of the shed, which left me alone up in the rafters. I sat down at the back end of the building and waited. Then I heard footsteps; someone was entering the building. From my position I was unable to see who it was. The footsteps seemed to be going to the back of the building. I was nervous as I crawled around and I called out Anthony's name. There was no response. I was getting really anxious."

Scott jumped down at that point, sure that Anthony was beneath the building playing a joke on him. He rushed outside. Anthony was up at the house, using the walkie talkie. Scott's thoughts went to Jerome. What was he looking for?

Other stories have been related to Scott, stories of eerie haunting at Calhoun Lodge. "One person told me that while fishing down by Blackstone Bay he could have sworn he heard fiddle music. However, no fiddler was in view by the shores of Calhoun Lodge. Other people have also mentioned hearing fiddle music as they canoed past the lodge."

In 1996 Scott and three other park employees actually heard Jerome speak. "The four of us were staying overnight in Jerome's old bedroom. We were all lying in our beds telling jokes, which were followed by a tremendous amount of laughter. When the jokes stopped, silence followed. It was time to sleep. Then we heard someone else laugh! Everyone was shocked and began to accuse one another. They thought I did it." Apparently Jerome enjoys a good joke, too.

In 1997 two park employees, Kevin and Kris, stayed in Jerome's old bedroom in the caretaker's house. As they lay in their bunks, sharing stories of the day, Kevin saw something just outside the open bedroom door, at the top of the stairs. What on earth was it? Kevin described it as a white mass of light in the shape of a man. Sure that this was all a bad dream, Kevin watched as the spirit floated through the doorway and stopped at the foot of his bed. Unable to speak or believe his eyes he rubbed them to clear his vision and then looked again. The figure was still there. Slowly the figure faded. Kevin said the ghost just vanished within itself.

Then Kris spoke up. "Did you see that?"

Kevin and Kris both agreed that the ghostly figure appeared to be a skinny form at the top of the stairs and increased in size as it entered the room. Scott thinks that Kevin and Kris saw Jerome; he believes Jerome still resides in that house.

Scott enjoys the romance of the ghost and celebrates it with poetry and song. If you decide to camp at Massasauga Park you could seek him out. Instead of the violin of Jerome drifting over the water it could be Scott singing "The Balad of Jereome Cascanette."

Please note that shortly after the publication of this story I was contacted by a family member of Jerome Cascanette. They told me that the family believes Jerome was murdered. According to them the maintenance shed in which he had been found had been locked from the outside!

Ojibway Hotel

~ Pointe-au-Baril ~

A woman dressed in white slowly drifts down the third floor of the majestic Ojibway Hotel. Her delicate feet barely touch the knotted pine floor. Her vacant eyes stare down the hall. She is not looking for anything. In fact, she found what she sought a long time ago. It was a dream come true — a dream that turned into a nightmare. As the sun dipped beneath the waters of Georgian Bay she watched from a chair in the tower. A short brown rope dangled beside her. She resolved to end her torment, but she has never left the Ojibway.

The hexagonal tower, the extended dining room wing, and the long roofed verandah help to create a luxurious, yet rustic, resort. The Ojibway Hotel was erected on a forty-two-acre island in the cottage area of Pointe-au-Baril in 1906. The original building, opened by Hamilton C. Davis of Rochester, New York, in 1907, was a plain wooden structure. Further additions on either side were added in 1910.

A plaque outside the hotel reads:

> At the turn of the century in a sparsely settled wilderness,
> Hamilton C. Davis built the Ojibway Hotel, opening this

magnificent sweep of Georgian Bay to women in long dresses and men in straw hats and spats who rode in long wooden launches and enjoyed the summer pleasures of the day.

The Ojibway Hotel boosted the economy in an otherwise sparsely employed area. Summer staff arrived from Parry Sound and the Shawanaga Reserve each summer. Mr. Davis imported students from the University of Rochester. Charles F. Cole worked there in 1922. "I was discovered by Hamilton C. Davis, who recruited me from the freshman class to wrestle with luggage as a bellhop, and to play for dances and beguile the ladies with soothing melodies in the hotel living room." The summer staff all resided on the island, with the Shawanaga families camped in tents some distance away.

The resort soon attracted the attention of nearby islanders. Mr. Davis catered to their needs with a post office, a grocery store, a hardware store, a repair shop, and an icehouse. Area residents and guests could even have their clothes cleaned in the steam laundry directly behind the hotel, a mere hop from the tower.

Collection of Ruth McCuaig

The Ojibway Hotel.

Ruth H. McCuaig, a lifelong resident of the Ojibway Hotel, recalls the interior of the main building in her book *Our Pointe Au Baril*:

> The interior remains much the same. Rough cedar posts support the ceilings of the two main ground-floor areas, there are large stone fireplaces in each, and one in the office lobby. Unpeeled white birch forms the railings of the stairways to the upper floors. Only the tower rooms, the most expansive, boasted private bathrooms. Bedrooms were sparsely furnished with plain cots, heavy white bedspreads, a dresser and a chair to two. People did not expect to spend much time in their rooms. For reading or writing letters, they could seek solitude in one of the few, open summerhouses or gazebos overlooking the water.

Eighty-five-year-old Ruth agreed to talk about the hotel. She very charmingly told me her memories. "The dining-room tables were set in keeping with the Ojibway theme — birchbark placemats, coasters, and napkin rings, all with quill motifs and sweetgrass borders. For a brief period some of the waitresses were even dressed in Native costume."

Hotel guests spent their days fishing or canoeing in the morning. Swimming was a pleasure and dinner an opportunity to dress. Ruth describes the attire: "Elaborate, fussy clothing was frowned on, but good-looking skirts and blouses, or simply summer dresses, silk stockings, and white shoes were the order of the day for women. Summer flannels, or light duck trousers, shirts, ties, and jackets or blazers were worn by the men. Bare feet would have been scorned."

Today the upper floors of the hotel structure are closed. The lounge and dining room are still used and a snack bar was installed in the former kitchen area. Cottagers still use the post office, grocery store, gift shop, and gas dock.

The island scenery, then as now, stirs the emotions. Romance is in the air. Warm, moonlit nights and dancing waters mean hearts can connect. On such an evening in the 1920s, a young, attractive American woman, who worked as a chambermaid, discovered love. He was a handsome, smooth-talking fellow.

The family clan strike an amusing pose before attending dinner. Suit jackets and dresses highlight the summer fashion of 1922. Men never went fishing on the bay without wearing a tie.

Dockside at the Ojibway Hotel.

As the story goes, she went in search of him one night. He was nowhere to be found. He had not arrived for their usual tryst on the far side of the island. She returned to her quarters on the third floor in the east wing. There she succumbed to tears. A dreadful thought persisted. He had shown some interest in a female guest. Could it be?

She had to know. Stealthily she made her way to the tower room and at the door she heard his voice. In she went and there they were — entwined in a passionate embrace. She fled in horror.

At dusk the next day she waited for the tower room to empty. With a chair from the desk she reached to the rafters and tied a rope; with the noose around her neck she faced the setting sun and kicked the chair away. A dramatic end for her and her nightmare.

Here in the Ojibway Hotel she remains, a white, veiled figure. The young summer employees see her so often they have named her the White Lady. The sightings usually occur in the third-floor tower room where she took her life and in the east-wing room she once inhabited. Her spirit usually appears at the end of the day.

However, Ruth McCuaig is adamant that no suicide ever occurred at the hotel. "I knew Hamilton Davis and have spent sixty years in the area. At no time was there ever any mention of a woman hanging herself in the tower room."

"I saw her," said John Cameron, office manager of the Ojibway. "A friend and I were in the process of closing up the building down by the dock one night. As we were walking up the front steps to the hotel we both glanced up at the tower. There she was, standing in the window, staring out at the water. She appeared to be in her early thirties and about medium height with shoulder-length hair. My friend made a hasty retreat and she vanished."

No one seems to know the woman's name. Everyone at the hotel is aware of the haunting, but has no specific knowledge of the characters involved. A suicide in a popular hotel in the 1920s would have been quickly covered up, unseemly to discuss and bad for business. No one wants to occupy a room where someone has committed suicide. Haunted hotels were not in vogue as they are today.

Three years ago Christian Dempsey was an employee at the Ojibway. He was returning to the hotel at dusk one evening and entered the front of the building to attend to the snack bar. Later he left the building through the back entrance. Just as he stepped outside he looked up at the back of the hotel and caught sight of the white-veiled woman looking out of her old east-wing room on the third floor.

Ed Kernaghan worked at the hotel four years ago and he seems to believe in the presence of a spirit at the hotel. According to John, Ed once offered to pay $500 to anyone willing to stay overnight in the tower room. No one ever took him up on his offer.

In 1995 a terrible storm struck the islands off Pointe-au-Baril. John recalls losing power to the resort. The entire complex was in darkness. John said, "One staff member went outside to watch the storm and to his amazement a light was on in the tower room!"

John often works late at night in the administration office in the second-floor tower room. His dog, who usually accompanies him, doesn't leave his side while they are in the tower room. No one wants to be the last person to leave, either.

The White Lady peers from the tower window of the Ojibway Hotel, captured on videotape by Rick Omahen of New York. He panned the Ojibway with his camcorder while on a boat cruise and, to his surprise, caught her image. Seconds later she disappeared.

Paul Lloyd is head of maintenance and lives there alone from mid-September to the end of November. Talking to him, I was reminded of *The Shining*, Stephen King's novel about a hotel caretaker whose soul is overtaken by a spirit. Paul opines, "When you live here alone you have to get a handle on things. I don't let my mind get out of control. I have to function. If you hear a noise your imagination can do anything. I have to live here." Paul does not deny the existence of the White Lady, but needs to avoid contact.

Her presence is strong in the east-wing room and in the tower. Most of the rooms are locked and the hallway furnishings are gone. If feels as though she will appear any moment.

Caley Hall is a young woman who works at the Ojibway. She would never stay alone in the hotel at night. "I've been coming up here since I was a child. I have often heard moaning and cries from the third floor." She knows there is a woman haunting the tower room.

The Ojibway is still an incredible place of beauty. Gone are the long dresses and the straw hats, the fishing guides and the steamers. But a woman remains behind to remind us of the past.

Two years ago Bruce Bishop, owner of Pleasant Cove Fishing Resort in Pointe-au-Baril, was conducting a boat tour of the islands, as he often does. When he arrived at the Ojibway Hotel, he told his guests about the woman who haunts the tower window. One guest on board used his camcorder to pan the entire hotel, even the tower. It never occurred to him to review it then, but when he did at home there she was, standing in the window.

Bungalow Camp

~ French River ~

A young woman disembarks at the train station. Her hair is covered by a scarf and she is wearing big, dark glasses. She hunches over slightly as she walks. No one would guess her real identity. However, the owner of the local lodge, Clarence Honey, does recognize her. "Hello, Miss Monroe, so nice to see you again. Please step this way and I'll get your bags."

And who was she really? Was she a Proust-reading sex kitten or was she a frightened child, caught up in the unforgiving world of Hollywood?

People who knew Marilyn well claimed she could turn on her Marilyn persona at will. She could appear in public unnoticed and suddenly lift her head, straighten her posture, flash her smile, toss her hair, and become the glorious Marilyn Monroe.

Shelly Winters, who shared an apartment with Marilyn early in her career, said, "She'd come out of our apartment in a shleppy old coat, looking like my maid, and all the people would push her aside to get my autograph. She loved it."

It proved to be hard work, turning this persona on and off, and it must have been even harder knowing when to flip the switch.

The French River Railway Station in the village of French River. People report hearing a ghost train travelling through here at night!

The late, great director Billy Wilder directed Marilyn twice, in *The Seven Year Itch*, when her marriage to Joe DiMaggio was falling apart, and in *Some Like It Hot*, when she and Arthur Miller were having marital problems. He said, "One side of Marilyn was wonderful, and the other side was terrible. She was two of a kind."

Marilyn was a Gemini and called herself, "Jekyll and Hyde. Two in one." She said, "I think when you are famous every weakness is exaggerated."

How heartbreaking it must have been to know that you must always, ultimately, disappoint those you love, including, of course, your legions of fans. And love her they did, although during her lifetime it was often a guilty pleasure. Marilyn was largely a figure of either lust or scorn.

In the 1950s Marilyn Monroe was considered shocking. She was a sensation and everything she did or wore created huge interest. Church officials advised their congregations not to see her movies, even though the clothing she wore in them was carefully censored: her shorts must not be too short, her dresses not cut too low. Joan Crawford openly criticized her wardrobe and called her a tart. The press delighted in describing her walk: Did she exaggerate the swing of her hips by trimming the heel of only one shoe? Had one hip been dislocated?

Through it all, Marilyn appeared innocent and slightly oblivious, as she couldn't quite comprehend what all the fuss was about. Pauline Kael explained this facade by calling her "baby whore." In keeping with this persona, Marilyn would give innocent answers to tawdry questions. "I learned to walk early and I've been doing it ever since," or "What do I have on when I go to bed? Why, the radio, of course."

But that was the screen Marilyn. The real Marilyn had to make a life for herself, away from the image that had been created.

Allan "Whitey" Snyder, Marilyn's devoted makeup man, said, "She had the greatest inferiority complex of any person I ever knew.... She's frightened to death of the public who think she is so sexy. My God, if they only knew how hard it is for her."

Marilyn Monroe made two movies in Canada. *Niagara*, with Joseph Cotton and Jean Peters, was filmed in Niagara Falls, Ontario, and New York in the summer of 1952 and released in January 1953. *River of No Return*, with Robert Mitchum and Rory Calhoun, was filmed in Jasper National Park in Alberta during the summer of 1953 and released in 1954.

Late in 1954 she endured a hospital stay and, as the press recorded, openly broke down as she was being discharged. That December she separated with Joe DiMaggio. Nineteen fifty-five was to be the start of a new life for her. That January she formed her own company with the photographer Milton Greene. She was one of the first movie starts to try to control her own career. She said at the time that she was going to change her whole life and the public's attitude to her by acting in important plays and writing poetry.

Marilyn wanted to be taken seriously. She knew what we came to know later: she was a gifted actress and talented comedienne. Yet, in June of that year *The Seven Year Itch* premiered, with images of a flirtatious, bubble-headed Marilyn, her skirt billowing over her shoulders. That scene, incidentally, also marked the end of her marriage to Joe DiMaggio.

Between June and December of 1955, when she signed a contract with 20th Century Fox, she was not filming and desperately needed time off. She escaped to Ontario in the fall. We have no way of knowing how often she visited Northern Ontario, but people in French River recall another visit from Marilyn in the summer of 1958. This would be consistent with her wish to get healthy — on July 8 she arrived in New York

City from California and happily confessed to the awaiting press that she was "overweight." On August 28 she announced her pregnancy. She and her husband, Arthur Miller, were jubilant at the prospect of a baby.

Shortly after the announcement she was on the set of *Some Like It Hot* for nine weeks. Her co-stars and the director of this film have said she was in terrible shape emotionally. During the shoot, she had to be hospitalized at one point for "nerves." She then returned to New York City on November 23, and on December 16 the news of her miscarriage became public. Marilyn's mental state worsened throughout the new year, and in June 1959 she had a medical procedure done that she hoped would prevent future miscarriages.

She stayed out of the public eye until that fall. During that time she would have had the opportunity to go north to the French River again.

In 1960, Marilyn found herself in a complex relationship with Yves Montand, the late French movie star. He and his wife, the late Simone Signoret (who, ironically, had just won an Oscar for her role as an abandoned, suicidal mistress in *A Room at the Top*), became great friends with Marilyn and Arthur Miller. They had adjacent bungalows at the Beverly Hills Hotel and dined together every night during the shooting of *Let's Make Love*, the movie Marilyn made with Mr. Montand.

Alas, the lives of celebrities are never their own — Marilyn's life is a perfect example — and separations are unavoidable. Ms. Signoret and Mr. Miller had commitments elsewhere and Marilyn and Yves Montand were left alone together.

Their love affair was a disaster for Marilyn. When Yves Montand returned to Europe he said, "If Marilyn hadn't been such a baby, there wouldn't have been so much gossip."

Simone Signoret, of course, distanced herself from Marilyn, although she had the intellect and understanding to give this affair the importance it deserved. In her wonderful book *Nostalgia Isn't What It Used to Be*, she wrote lovingly of her relationship with Marilyn and said she treasured a scarf Marilyn gave her. Although it was frayed at one edge, she simply turned that edge in to hide the flaw, undoubtedly a metaphor for a flaw in Marilyn that Ms. Signoret chose to forgive.

Marilyn's reaction to the end of the affair was not as sanguine. In June she overdosed on sleeping pills. In July she travelled to Nevada to begin filming *The Misfits*, written for her by her husband, and she arrived dishevelled and ungroomed. The press had a field day describing her confused and weary condition.

In August she overdosed again on barbiturates. She was hospitalized and when filming of *The Misfits* ended in the fall, she and Arthur Miller separated. Shortly after shooting ended Clark Gable, her co-star and father figure, died. There were accusations that Marilyn's behaviour on the set had precipitated his fatal heart attack. Not surprisingly, her mental state deteriorated disturbingly.

The following February she was hospitalized again, and was in and out of clinics and hospitals during 1961, as she was in and out of liaisons with John F. Kennedy, Frank Sinatra, and her former husband Joe DiMaggio. She also learned that another ex-husband, Arthur Miller, had married the talented Inge Morath, a photographer who was on the set of *The Misfits*.

Sometime during 1960 or early 1961 Marilyn began ingesting more powerful drugs. She travelled to Mexico in early 1962 where she acquired even more of them. As far as the press was concerned, it was open season on Marilyn. As her public behaviour became more bizarre and she was often obviously high or drunk or distressed by the media frenzy around her, the press became more aggressive. Marilyn Monroe's traumas were big news and sold newspapers and magazines and, of course, no matter how ill she became, she was always beautifully photogenic.

In March 1962, she was awarded the Golden Globe for her performance in *The Misfits*. The televised event did not include her acceptance as she was obviously incapacitated. Photos that appeared in the press show a droopy-eyed, vacuous beauty, kissing her wine glass or slumped against Rock Hudson, who presented her award.

By April she was shooting *Something's Got to Give* at the ailing 20th Century Fox studios. She took a break in May to make her famous appearance at John F. Kennedy's party to sing "Happy Birthday, Mr. President," a very public declaration of their romantic involvement. In all photos of that event, a discreet First Lady, Jacqueline Kennedy, is not to be seen. She apparently excused herself and returned when Marilyn departed.

Marilyn's illnesses stopped the shooting of *Something's Got to Give*, which was being shot on the studio lot since the excesses of *Cleopatra* left the studio financially strapped. In June 20th Century Fox fired her and stopped production of the film. People were put out of work, for which Marilyn was publicly blamed.

On August 5, 1962, the news of her death was reported. Conspiracy theories were rife and they still surface, however, her death was declared a suicide and was probably accidental. Marilyn had admitted to her friends that she had tried to commit suicide several times and said that suicide is "a person's privilege. I don't believe it's a sin or a crime. It's your right if you want to, though it doesn't get you anywhere."

Arthur Miller said, "Beneath all her insouciance and wit, death was her companion everywhere and at all times, and it may be that its acknowledged presence was what lent her poignancy, dancing at the edge of oblivion as she was."

Whitey Snyder made her up for the last time for her funeral. He had promised he would, in jest, and she reminded him with a money clip engraved

Whitey Dear, While I'm still warm, Marilyn.

There were many periods during her very stressful existence that she could have, and should have, gone to French River. Certainly the quiet surroundings, fresh air, and good, wholesome food would be a far cry from the life she led in Hollywood. We know more than once in the 1950s this troubled, anxious, and frail young woman sought sanctuary at the Bungalow Lodge.

She didn't need to be a star on the French River. She wasn't housed by press or fans. The people at the inn respected her privacy and understood her need for solitude. Why wouldn't she want to stay there forever?

The staff certainly think she has.

In 1923 Canadian Pacific Railway officials were looking for ways to increase passenger service on the line from Toronto to Sudbury. An elite tourist fishing resort was built on the French River at the hub of a maze of waterways, looking west toward the Recollet Falls. It was only eighty metres (two hundred yards) from the train station and offered self-contained suites, described in the company's brochure as:

> ... a cluster of charming rustic bungalows ... simple but abundantly comfortable, having ... running water,

electric light, and a spacious verandah ... the rates at French River Bungalow Camp are $5.00 per day, $30.00 per week, American plan.... A fast train leaves Toronto in the morning, giving connections from New York, Buffalo, Pittsburgh and Cleveland.

Bungalow Camp enjoyed many famous visitors over the years. In 1939, during the Royal Tour before the Second World War, King George VI and Queen Elizabeth enjoyed dinner in the main dining room and stayed in their private rail car on the property. In honour of this visit, the stonework in the dining room's fireplace was arranged in the shape of the king's crown. This feature is still intact.

In 1945 the property was sold to Clarence E. Honey, who operated it successfully until 1965. During the 1950s the camp gained a reputation as a retreat for several Hollywood celebrities. Clark Gable and Ray Bolger, known best for his role as the scarecrow in the *Wizard of Oz*, signed the guest register.

Marilyn Monroe, too, discovered Bungalow Camp and stayed in chalet 15. Locals there remember that she enjoyed the simple, rustic life,

Yesterdays' main lodge.

but she seemed nervous and on the verge of hysteria. She needed the peace this place could help to give her. Many of the workers at the lodge believe that has held her there.

Since 1965 the resort has changed hands several times, and has been renamed. In 1992 the place was named Yesterdays, a very appropriate name as the past does tend to linger there. There is a strange, quiet, and timeless feel to the place. The guests of the past seem to mingle with the guests of the present.

Larry and Janis Pichette now own and operate the resort, which features twenty-two chalets, a spacious dining room that can accommodate up to one hundred and fifty diners, a spa, tennis courts, recreation centre, and conference room. Janis is not shy about admitting the presence of unseen guests. She has had several experiences since 1995.

Does she believe Marilyn Monroe is still there? "I have heard it from too many people that she is really here. Guests see a beautiful blonde woman who appears and then immediately disappears.

"One Sunday night in the winter when we were closed I was all alone working in the office. Suddenly the door opened by itself. You could feel someone was there. Then I saw her. A vaporous form."

You may sit by the fire and hear music coming from some invisible source. Doors open as though someone is entering the main lodge. On occasion the coffee pot is emptied by some unseen visitor.

Andrea Lehman, a young housekeeper at the lodge, believes a spirit inhabits chalet 15. "When I am working in chalet fifteen, I can feel someone there with me, but no one ever appears to me. The person is over in the corner of the room."

Sandy Rancourt, another employee, told me about a couple who had been married at the lodge in 1946 and came back to celebrate their fiftieth wedding anniversary. "They stayed in chalet fifteen. The couple saw the apparition of a beautiful blonde woman, who appeared in front of them."

In that chalet, coffee stir sticks keep appearing on the floor. Staff replace them on the appropriate shelf, but when they return the sticks are on the floor again. They all believe Marilyn inhabits the lodge.

Sandy MacKean is the executive chef at the resort. He feels he is never alone in the kitchen, and gave me several examples of why he feels that way. "The coffeemaker will start on its own. You'll make a pot of coffee and then come back and discover that someone has drunk three quarters of the pot." Marilyn especially loved coffee; it was her favourite drink, after *Dom Pérignon* champagne.

"The door by the kitchen wait station will swing wide open and then shut on its own. I have even seen a shadow go by. I thought it was one of the staff, until I realized I was all alone. I tried to turn the stove on and it was already going. I have heard the walk-in fridge door open and close. Utensils and pots rattle in the kitchen when no one is there."

The staff working in the dining room often see a shadow following behind them. It is not unusual to find the silverware rearranged on the tables. Staff members Pam Couvrette and Nathalie Joncas have both heard their names called by a woman several times.

Nathalie told me, "Sometimes I will be sitting by the fireplace and I will hear a woman singing.

"I [was sitting] in a wing chair in the lobby at 5:00 p.m. ... glasses hanging over the bar in the lobby area began to rattle against one another. All the staff agree that there is more paranormal activity late in the day and at night."

The week after my visit with Janis and the staff, the activity increased significantly. The abundance of paranormal activity included an apparition in the dining room, the kitchen door to the outside opened and closed on its own, the telephone system went crazy, and the cash register decided to tally its own figures. There has never been so much activity during such a short time.

Marilyn certainly wouldn't have stayed in Hollywood. She once said, "Hollywood is a place where they'll pay your a thousand dollars for a kiss and fifty cents for your soul. I know, because I turned down the first offer often enough and held out for the fifty cents."

Yesterdays really is aptly named. You can step out of time there. Your chance of having an experience with a guest of the past is high. One of them may be the restless spirit of Marilyn Monroe.

Since the writing of this story, Janis Pichette has passed away. Yesterdays is now closed to the public, having become the Enaahtig North Healing Lodge.

Time Travellers

The day was sunny and the waters calm, when a young couple headed out boating along the jagged rocky shoreline of Newfoundland. Their destination was a small fishing hamlet located a few miles to the south.

Everything seemed fine at first; however, a low fog bank began to roll in and the light quickly faded to grey. Minutes turned into hours. Fearing the worst, they wondered if they would simply pass the village without ever seeing it and vanish from sight. Just when all seemed lost, they saw it: a light shining in the window of a house on top of a bluff. They headed toward the light and found the channel that brought them in. When they docked they quickly related their story and the gratitude they felt for the light in the window. Blank stares soon revealed the truth. According to the locals, the house they had seen had burned down several years before. All that was left to mark the site was a foundation and a couple of gravestones nearby. Had the couple sailed into the fourth dimension?

We call time the fourth dimension. Most people are unfamiliar with the idea of stepping outside of time. When it does happen, people are usually not aware that they are experiencing anything out of the ordinary.

There are no gauges to help us here, no rules of the game. Time travel is simply a shift to another plane of consciousness and perception, where the present no longer exists and the past comes to life.

A person never sees their self in time. Maurice Nicoll writes, in *Psychological Commentaries on the Teachings of Gurdjieff and Ouspensky*, "We do not see the Time-Bodies of ourselves or of things. We think the past is dead. Our lives are living lines in living Time. Owing to our relation to Time, however, we see only a point in Time and then another, and we call them present moments."

In our physical life we are conscious of three dimensions of space — length, height, and depth or volume. What we don't see are other dimensions. For that we need the power of astral sight — to be able to see beyond the blindfold of beliefs and enter the world some people call the illusion.

In the fourth dimension objects and inhabitants are real in the same way as our own bodies, furniture, houses, or monuments. All we need to do is shed our perceived concept of time. We need to rid ourselves of the clock and function according to solar time. Think about dreams for a moment. During a dream we have no concept of time. A full dream can happen in a few minutes of ordinary time. We simply travel to wherever our dreams take us. When we wake up we have no recollection of time. Where did we go and for how long?

The veil of time is thin in many places, particularly in specific natural settings. Aboriginal elders have long eluded to these sacred places, calling them portals.

Most people are too uncomfortable to share any time experience for fear of ridicule. However, Ian Mollet was more than willing to share with us. Ian is a soft-spoken man who has lived his life in balance with the great outdoors. At the early age of five he would hunker down in a hand-fashioned fort in old furs while the wind howled around him. There he dreamed of times when men and women faced the elements and lived in simple ways. He believes he was once a *coureur de bois*.

"I have been a trailblazer since the age of five. That was when I made my first trail in the bush." Ian has the instinctive gift of finding direction without the aid of compass, sun, moon, or stars. He can look at a map then begin to travel from point A and arrive at point B without any navigational aids. His great-great-grandfather, who settled in Canada in the

1860s, was a visionary. He died at the age of eighty-nine, but knew there would be wars and depressions in the twentieth century.

Ian has another gift. He is able to enter the fourth dimension and travel back in time. His first clear recollection of this was an incident that occurred on a canoe and fishing trip back in the early 1980s. Keep in mind this river was a major fur-trading route in the seventeenth and eighteenth centuries. Ian and a group of father/son and father/daughter teams had rented some rustic cabins near Noëlville, by the French River. At about 5:00 p.m. one day, Ian and his good friend Ron decided to canoe a short distance west of the cabins, to a high rock on the south shore of the French River. Pulling up to shore, they disembarked and began to climb the eight metres (twenty-four feet) to the top. The view was spectacular. The men could see the river in both directions. A few cabins dotted the shoreline.

"We were sitting side by side on the rock. In tune and comfortable with one another, we sat there contemplating our own private thoughts. While I was sitting there a peculiar wave-like action happened to my vision. It was like a wind coming up on a body of calm water, causing the water to ripple. Suddenly the buildings along the river disappeared. The trees and river remained. I was back in the 1600s and I was indeed a *coureur de bois*. We were on our way to Georgian Bay. I was no longer aware of Ron. The configuration of the river was slightly different and the water was moving much faster. Then this ripple effect occurred again to my vision and I came back, wondering what the hell had just happened. Ron knew something was up and I explained it all to him as best I could."

Ian didn't have another experience like this until the early 1990s, when he and his wife were on a cruise ship out of Parry Sound. "We had just left the dock when this wave action happened again to my vision. At the time we were looking across the harbour, at the Sound Marina and the houses along the shoreline. Once again everything disappeared. I was back in the early 1600s. All the houses were gone and the forest touched the water's edge."

Ian has had other experiences of the paranormal. In 1983 he was in a hockey dressing room, talking to some people, when something very unusual happened to him. "I disappeared. I could hear the peoples' conversation, but I was above them. My body no longer existed. I was really above and beyond myself watching people having a conversation that only a few minutes before I had been part of."

Ian was also close to his father, who passed away in 1992. He hoped to see him in his dreams, but little did he expect what he got!

One day in 1997 he left work at lunch and went to the Georgian Inn, to work out in their gym. This was quite a common thing for Ian to do. As he walked downstairs and into the small change room he sensed he was not alone. "I turned around to take my shirt off and caught my reflection in the wall mirror. My face was my father's face. I felt the familiar wavy action occur with my vision. There I was looking at my father. I knew as long as I maintained eye contact with him he would remain. It seemed as though he wanted to relate something to me. His face was so calm, I got the feeling he was consoling me. Why was it going on so long? It was like watching something on video going from one segment to the other. When I glanced away he was gone."

A short time later, Ian was diagnosed with chronic lymphatic leukemia. He is still battling this today with all his remarkable physical and spiritual strength.

Ian also had a strange experience while in a meditation class in the 1980s. "One night I was sitting on the edge of my bed, meditating before going to sleep. Meditation helps me to prepare myself for a good night's sleep. When I was saying certain affirmations to myself I had the feeling that my mind wanted to take me somewhere. I decided to go with it. All of a sudden I was north of Mono Centre on the Bruce Trail, at the highest point in the area on an open-crowned hill. I was looking down the valley, viewing ponds and cliffs and trees. I was sitting on a rock and beside me was a friend whom I have known since I was ten years old. This friend would not normally be in the Bruce Trail area. He is a very devout Catholic and has very strong beliefs. I looked at my friend and said to him. 'This is my God,' while holding my hands out to the valley below. Immediately after I spoke, I levitated off the ground above him and started to fly very slowly down the valley. I was about three hundred and fifty metres [four hundred yards] above the ground.

"I remember heading south and then I started to accelerate. As I gained altitude I swung out through the stratosphere and into deep space. Now the planets and the stars began to whiz by me. I continued to go until I left this galaxy. I wondered where I was heading. I came not to darkness, nor to brightness. It was palpable gray that soon became light, and then I came to a full stop. I was at the centre of everything. Far more than any time in my life before or since I knew there was a God. I also immediately understood and knew everything I needed to know. About time, I knew at that point, that the past, the future, and the present are one. I knew the history of the world. I could understand the teachings of love. I could forgive people like Hitler for what they did — I knew it was right to forgive. I felt happy to have realized that. Then it happened. The whole experience overwhelmed me. My mind could not handle the experience. I became frightened. I came reeling back to the side of the bed. My head was pounding. What had just taken place?

"In that moment I was like an encyclopedia of knowledge concerning the history of mankind. I did not know what to do. The logical thing was to crawl into bed. I lay there with my eyes wide open. I woke up my wife, Pam, and described the entire experience to her. Then I felt much calmer. I sensed real peace for the first time in my life.

"For the next several days I maintained a working and living lifestyle that reflected this knowledge of forgiveness and acceptance. People began to respond positively to me. Ultimately, however, the enlightenment wore thin. I have tried many times to get back to that special place, but each time I have failed. I am still waiting."

Ian Mollet is not alone. Others have also experienced extraordinary journeys in time. It takes a kind of sensitivity to be open to the experience of ghosts. Here is a man who has experienced his father as a ghost, and also, in a way, himself.

Claudette Boyd, owner of Health Connections, a bookstore and alternative health counselling centre in Parry Sound, had an experience she related to me. One night a stranger came knocking at her door and Claudette filled more than a few pages in her journal when she left. "It was eight o'clock on a Sunday night in April. I heard a knock at the front door. A lady was standing on my doorstep. She said to me, 'I was just out to get some milk at the store and for some reason I knew I had to stop here and see if anyone was home.'"

She needed to talk to someone. She had heard about Claudette, but had never met her before. This stranger had arrived on Claudette's doorstep because she had a story to tell and was searching for some answers. "I sat down and listened to her. She began by telling me about an archaeological dig that took place near Collingwood. Apparently someone had found an ancient Native village. Her husband was associated with the archaeologist on the site and together they had decided to visit the dig. When they went to the site she experienced a different time. She was suddenly a young woman sitting in a circle of Native elders, including a medicine man. She also saw that she lived in the village near this medicine man. She was close to this holy man and appeared to be happy.

"She was married to a young brave who was killed in battle. The medicine man knew this was going to happen, but did nothing to prevent it. She discovered this and had come to hate the medicine man. Suddenly she knew she was back in the present with her husband. He was aware that something had happened to her. She did not want to leave the area. She knew she could return to that time as any moment. Her husband sensed her distress, walked her to their car, and took her out for ice cream! He placed a cone in her hand and that seemed to jolt her back to reality.

"She remembered the first time the medicine man had spoken directly to her. He had told her why he had not tried to prevent her young husband's death. She understood what he was saying but still felt anger toward him."

The woman asked Claudette what she should do with the experience. What did it all mean? Was this woman still carrying anger from another lifetime? Why could she not go back a second time? How does someone cope with such an experience? Who would believe her?

The experience was real to her. Certainly a message was delivered. Perhaps this is why she could not return a second time. The difficulty is in believing that it has actually happened and then in finding someone to listen to your story and help you to understand its meaning.

A ghost appears in the present but comes from the past. If we travel back in time do we become a ghost of the future? When a ghost is attached to a person and travels with them wherever they go, what does that say about space? Ottilie Hubmann has a forty-year personal haunting to share.

Ottilie is quite a remarkable person. She is awake in this lifetime. Her earliest memory is from the age of six months, lying in a wicker basket and listening to her older brother crying. She remembers thinking, "Why is he so worried?" It was wartime, and Ottilie's parents had abandoned their children in Munich, Germany. They were alone.

Ottilie Hubmann.

Her next strong memory was at the age of two, when she had the thought, "Why am I here in an orphanage? I don't belong here!" Shortly afterward she was adopted.

A childhood experience has been her lifelong guiding light. She explains, "When I was four years old, living with step-parents, I remember standing in front of a large mirror in the entranceway and looking at myself and asking 'Who am I?' I knew at that moment that I could just go. I was not limited to the physical body. I could leave this body at any time. At that moment I remembered I am spirit, not body. I still get goosebumps relating this story. I was searching for the spiritual. I think an experience like this is important to you. It helps to lead the way."

Being open to spirit also allows you to see what others cannot. As a young girl Ottilie recalls lying in bed and seeing the shadow of a body out of the corner of her eye. She also saw sparks in the air. At sixteen she came face to face with this shadow. It was a frightening and shocking experience for one who was so young, innocent, and quite alone with the experience.

"At age sixteen I was still living in Munich. I was very shy and innocent. It was in the morning in my bedroom when I woke up to a man standing at the entrance to my room. He was of average height, wearing a black, hooded cloak and brandishing a knife. The only part of his face you could see was his lips. They were bright red. As he approached me, he suddenly vanished into thin air. He appeared to be quite vicious."

This black-cloaked figure would only appear when Ottilie was experiencing some stress, and always in her bedroom. In the first year he appeared five times. Sometimes he even seemed as though he wanted to strangle her.

At age twenty-three she left Munich for South Africa. She had a sense of relief, knowing she would never again see this hideous figure that had haunted her youth. "I moved to a place with a large bay window. One morning I awoke to a dazzling sunrise. All of a sudden I saw a pair of hands opening the window from the outside. I froze with fear.

This was a bad dream. He was back. I watched him climb through the window and approach my bed. Then he disappeared.

"I didn't know what to do. I couldn't talk to anyone. He always appeared in the morning. Sometimes he came through the window and other times through the doorway. He never spoke a word. I always felt evil. He never walked through a wall. He was as real as you or I."

Three years later, Ottilie moved back to Germany and he followed her once again. As a matter of fact, each time she moved, he moved. There was nothing she could do. Inevitably, he would show up.

In 1982 she moved to Parry Sound, Ontario, with her husband. Within the first month he appeared. This spirit seemed to have no problem crossing continents. This time, however, he came much closer to her. "He was about one and a half metres [four feet] from me. I saw his eyes. They were quite normal looking. Finally I had enough. I shouted at him: 'Go! I am not afraid of you. I don't want to see you anymore.' It worked, he disappeared and I never saw him again. That is, until the late 1980s, when I decided to travel to New Mexico to a conference on past-life regression.

"I wanted to know what my soul's journey was. For the first few days at the conference we meditated and each worked with a facilitator. One day I told my facilitator that I was feeling quite depressed. This is quite unusual, since I am always a very happy person. I felt like I had a black cloud hovering over me. He had me lie down and he stood behind me. He told me that when I breathed in I was to ask for a symbol.

"The symbol I saw for myself was a ballpoint pen. I was disappointed. After all, they didn't have ballpoint pens in the past. How could this be a symbol for my higher self? However, I followed the instructions and soon a picture appeared. I was in a chamber in a castle. It was a torture chamber. *Here comes my bad past*, I thought. I was the victim.

"My facilitator wanted to close the session after relating this to him. Yet, I really believed something was about to happen. We kept going. Then he appeared. The black-cloaked figure, who I had not seen in a number of years. He was in the torture chamber with me, holding a book open in one hand and a quill pen in the other. There was my symbol, the ballpoint pen. I could feel him, and I knew everything that he was thinking. This was the man who was responsible for signing my death warrant. He was feeling guilty that he had not saved my life. He had become emotionally attached to me.

Ian Mollet.

"We then sent him love. Please go to the light. I took his hand and we walked to the light. Go on to the light. He entered the light and disappeared. I knew he was gone for good."

Ottilie has not seen him since, but he was certainly with her for many years.

Each of these three stories seemed like an illusion to the participant. However, Ian Mollet did see the landscape change in front of him. When he looked into the mirror, his face did become his father's face. Was it just a coincidence that Ian became ill with cancer shortly afterward? And what about his journey during meditation when he stepped outside of time and shifted to another place of insight? It was real enough to change his outlook on life.

The woman at Claudette's door needed to tell her story. She needed someone to believe her. The time portal she entered is well-known to Aboriginal elders. Was it a coincidence that her husband knew the archaeologist? Aboriginal peoples have always connected with their ancestors to help them make present-day decisions that will affect their tomorrows. Visions of past events are part of that sacred medicine.

Ottilie Hubmann's early childhood memories indicate an aware spirit.

How do we unlock the mystery of time, the movement of the fourth dimension, or reality? When does it come to each person's aid? What beacons of light have any of us had and not recognized as being out of ordinary time? Have we found other ways to explain them or have we suppressed them out of fear?

Adamson Estate

~ Mississauga ~

You never know what you might find in the attic. When Anthony Adamson went looking he unlocked the very soul of his lineage. It wasn't the mummy's hand or locks of Victorian hair that disturbed his sight; it was the sudden release of energy that had been imprinted and bound in trunks and diaries and letters for decade upon decade. Anthony's snooping seems to have restored the Adamson Estate to life, and it has remained so ever since!

For years rumours have persisted that the Adamson Estate, on the shores of Lake Ontario in Port Credit, is haunted. The Adamson family story is an intense and emotional one; a story that has perhaps bound them to their estate, forever. Money, love, greed, and attachment are key ingredients for troubled tales involving the past, present, and future of places. Powerful life forces never seem to vanish under such spells.

The story begins in 1809, when loyalist Joseph Cawthra received a two hundred-acre land grant in the area now known as Port Credit. At the time, Cawthra purchased an additional two hundred acres, adjoining the granted property.

The deed required that Joseph erect a house and settle on the land within three years of receiving the grant. Joseph, accordingly, built a log cabin near the shoreline of Lake Ontario.

On December 13, 1864, John Cawthra, the grandson of Joseph, married Elizabeth Jane Elwell, the daughter of a deceased professional gentleman. John was forty years of age and Elizabeth a mere teenager.

In 1866 John and two of his brothers, Henry and Joseph, divided the original Cawthra lands. John took ownership of forty acres on the lake with the log cabin, Henry obtained one hundred acres on Lake Ontario, and Joseph received one hundred acres north of the Lakeshore Road. John built a two-storey summer home for his wife on his property, to which he later added a one-storey kitchen wing. The house design was inspired by the private hotel in Switzerland where he and his wife had met. It was built at the very edge of Lake Ontario in a grove of pine trees, which generated the name Grove Farm.

In 1870 a bank barn was raised. The base was constructed from Credit River stone. By 1871 Frank and Mary Duck had moved into the gardener's cottage that stood near the front gates. The Duck family oversaw the maintenance and operation of Grove Farm, a position they held until 1885, when the Richie family replaced them.

John Cawthra died on February 11, 1875, when Elizabeth was twenty-nine years old. The couple had three children, Elwell, Bertie, and Mabel. Elizabeth's life is detailed in a book by her grandson, Anthony Adamson, called *Wasps in the Attic*. Family lore has it that after her husband's death, Elizabeth received constant proposals. She had no real need for the financial support of a husband, and no wish to be tied irrevocably to a husband with a career in Toronto. Her greatest desire in life was to travel.

In the 1890s everybody who was anybody in Toronto went "'round the world." Elizabeth and her daughter Mabel set out on October 13, 1890, to travel around the world for eighteen months. Mabel had just received her share of her father's inheritance, on her twenty-first birthday. The money was enough to give her independence and freedom to do as she wished. She had been schooled at Brighton College, in England, and by governesses at the various foreign resorts to which her mother took her. She was very creative and became involved in the arts. Mabel was an agnostic and headstrong, not to mention a feminist. Despite her good looks and rich auburn hair, she was never a society belle.

Mabel was attractive to men for many reasons: her character, her accomplishments, her looks, and, of course, her money. Mabel was probably the one who brought home the mummy's hand from her travels around the world.

While searching the attic for clues to his mother's personality, Anthony discovered a bundle of sixty-three letters written by Mabel (his mother) to Agar Adamson (his father). Anthony shared some of his findings. "My parents had presumably known each other since 1894, but Agar Adamson was not mentioned until September 27, 1895. On March 17, 1895, Mabel confided to Agar that she was secretly engaged to a Captain Sparkes, but that he would not be eligible for advancement if he were to marry."

Agar was apparently in love with Mabel, and Anthony believes they became engaged in August of 1899. The couple planned to honeymoon in Mexico.

In a letter dated October 26, 1899, Mabel revealed her attitude to life and marriage to Agar.

> Your dear letter full of love and trust puts me to shame — I have such a terror of settling down. I hate doing anything irrevocable and I want you to feel that marriage is not the hard and fast, hopelessly binding thing that most people think it is. I don't feel that it is, I am simply going to live with you because I want to and if I cease to want to I shall leave and hope that you will do the same.

In Toronto, on November 15, 1899, at St. George's Church, the Reverend Canon Cayley married Mabel and Agar.

In 1900 Agar received a captaincy and left for South Africa to fight in the Boer War. In his absence, Mabel gave birth to a twelve-pound baby boy. They called him Rodney. Five years later, Anthony Adamson was born.

Anthony described his childhood: "Summer life at Port Credit was glorious. The house or cottage was small. To accommodate children, visitors, gardening tools, and a motorcar, a separate building was erected. This structure was unique in that the roadway to the house proper ran under an archway through the middle of the building. It also had a bell in a bell cote."

The building Anthony described was the gatehouse, constructed in 1904, which the family considered a folly. The word *folly* usually refers to an ornamental building. This particular one is believed to be the only wooden gatehouse of its kind in Canada.

In August of 1914, Agar Adamson went to fight in the First World War. Mabel, then forty-five, was determined that if she could help it she was not going to stay home and keep house and look after children while her husband went to war. She left in October for England, taking Anthony and leaving Rodney in the care of his Uncle Bertie.

Agar wrote a letter to Mabel almost every day of the war. He graphically described the emotional, mental, and physical stress of the soldiers.

February 18, 1915
… military discipline very severe … several men have been shot for straying away from camp.

March 2, 1915
There was only one rifle working owing to mud … at 6:30 a.m. I gave the signal to start back and one by one they crawled to a ditch 100 yards away … in places six feet deep in water full of dead bodies including horses … the Germans eventually saw us crawling …some of the men not able to swim … we never had more than twenty-eight in the "trench"at a time.

March 4, 1915
I found opium was a great effect in relieving wounded men … it is very difficult dressing a wounded man in a bombarded trench … impossible to take clothes off … you cut with a knife and pour iodine … often impossible to see … the moon helps … send scissors.

March 23, 1915
The men have not had a bath or a change of underclothes since the 26 of February.

Anthony wrote, "The decade of the 1920s had its traumas for many families. The after effect of the First World War was all pervading, and both my parents, in their separate ways, were war casualties. The effect of four years of mud and corpses had left my father impatient and irritable when things were not as he wanted them. He could not be driven fast in traffic and would quarrel with taxi drivers. He could blow up in a restaurant if there was any delay in service.

"Family dislocation, rows with her brother over money, and the erratic behaviour of her elder son, combined, as it was, with the running of a personal relief organization in Belgium, had left my mother physically ill and mentally distressed. She found her husband still devoted to her but not really the same man. He had some of the characteristics of an unexploded bomb ... she could not take it and she was beginning to not be able to afford it. She thought he ought to be occupied at some job.

"My mother went to Canada in the fall of 1919, leaving her family in England. She had decided that the place in which she and her husband and children had been the happiest was Grove Farm."

Mabel decided they needed a new house. She hired Sproatt and Rolfe, a Toronto architectural firm, to design a stucco-covered brick house with Flemish gables and a front door that, when opened, would look right out over Lake Ontario. She wanted the design delivered within a week. They produced one that she liked and she asked them to have it ready for occupancy by the spring of 1920. They said this was not possible, so she paid them for the plans and hired Robert Irvine of the Thornton Smith Company, who accomplished the feat. Upon completion of the house, the other summer cottage was torn down.

Anthony described his parents growing estrangement: "She [Mabel] did not die for another twenty-five years, but the beautiful new house at Port Credit, her regained health, and Agar's survival were not enough to keep them together.

"They shared their summers from 1921 till 1926 at Port Credit."

A letter of hers, written to Agar on May 11, 1927, stated,

> I am not to be cajoled any more. I think if you compare the life you lead when alone, to the life I lead when

alone, you will notice that they have very little in common and therefore it would be very foolish of us to try to live together. We don't even speak the same language.

To supplement his income, Agar had been selling the family silver.

In October of 1929, Agar flew in an experimental plane, with a famous British aviator, to Ireland. The plane fell into the Irish Sea and they floated for two hours before they were picked up by a trawler. The ordeal nearly did Agar in. And when his prostate needed attention soon after he was in no condition to withstand an operation.

Anthony was studying in England at the time. Mabel was in Canada. She arrived the day before Agar died. Anthony stated, "She was elegant and carefully dressed, and in no hurry. When we got to his room he was already breathing stertorously. I placed the oxygen mask over his face. He soon stopped breathing. My mother, who was standing, said quite simply, and without tears, 'That's it! Will you go downstairs and deal with it?'

"In the British caste system, undertakers are not gentlemen. We went together to an undertaker and proceeded down an old wooden stair to a basement filled with coffins on trestles, some empty, some full. It was not refrigerated. We wanted 'Adamson.' The undertaker took out a reference book and opened a coffin. She looked at him silently and then said, 'It is a beautiful face, isn't it.'

"His body was cremated and his ashes were put in my leather top-hat box and we both set sail for Canada." Mabel arranged a military funeral. Agar was buried in the Trinity Church yard beside the Credit River.

It was time for Anthony to begin a new life for himself. He fell in love with Charlotte Augusta Bonnycastle and they were married in 1931.

Anthony had been primarily educated in England and trained as an architect at Cambridge. He had just been accepted as a member of the new Ontario Association of Architects and had set up a partnership with another architect, Eric Arthur, who later became well-known for his work in architectural history. Anthony later became a professor of architecture at the University of Toronto.

The year he was married, Anthony decided to design a house for himself and his bride, on the grounds of Grove Farm. The house would be a statement of his skill as an architect. It was a unique and elegant building that featured the practical simplicity of the international styles of the 1930s, along with classical proportion of detailing.

Anthony and Augusta moved into the house in 1832. Their first son, Adrian Cawthra Adamson, was born in January 1933. A second son, named Inigo Thomas Herbert Cawthra Adamson, arrived in May of 1935.

By 1942 Mabel had developed multiple sclerosis and was losing her ability to walk. She returned to Port Credit for the summer of 1943. In the fall of the same year, Mabel became ill and died of pneumonia. She was buried, along with the ashes of her husband, in a vault designed by Anthony and erected in the yard of Trinity Church on the Credit River.

After his mother's death, Anthony and his family moved into the big house. His own house was then rented to their friends Duncan and Alice Derry. By the mid 1940s the Derry family had purchased the house, and it became known as the Derry House. They owned it for more than fifty years, until it was acquired by the city of Mississauga in 1997. Sunday, September 9, 2001, marked the beginning of an exciting new chapter, when the Derry House opened as a joint project of the Mississauga Shrine Club, St. John Ambulance, and the Multiple Sclerosis Society of Canada. The house is now used as office space for these organizations and the operation of numerous programs.

Mable's other son, Rodney, managed to get the Conservative nomination for West Toronto and in the subsequent election he defeated the Liberal incumbent and began a seventeen-year career as a member of Parliament.

In 1954 Rodney and his second wife died in a plane crash over Moose Jaw. A training plane crashed into their Trans-Canada Airlines plane and everyone on board perished.

By the 1960s, Anthony and his wife had moved to Rosedale, in Toronto. They rented out the Adamson house at Grove Farm. Anthony planned to develop a subdivision at Grove Farm during the seventies, which would have meant the destruction of the Adamson House, the gatehouse, and the barn. But perhaps his ancestors were protecting their estate. Instead of being developed, the property was expropriated by the Credit Valley Conservation Authority in 1975 and turned into a park. The city of Mississauga leased the Adamson House, and it eventually became home to the Royal Conservatory of Music. The Adamson House and gatehouse were designated historic sites, ensuring that they will remain protected for a long time — perhaps forever.

The Adamson Estate has a very strong energy. There is a constant feeling of being watched. There seems to be several different spirits here.

I first visited the estate with Matthew Wilkinson, an historian with the Mississauga Foundation. The moment I got out of the car I was struck by the tranquil energy and picturesque setting of the estate. It felt like a place where one could go to heal emotional distress or to contemplate life. The setting is truly restful. No wonder Mabel was anxious to return there. The estate was her sanctuary and in that setting she had hoped to save her marriage.

As we strolled to the front of the house, facing Lake Ontario, Matthew drew my attention to the gatehouse and related what he had heard about the apparition that is associated with the structure. Apparently there was a groundskeeper living on the estate when the First World War broke out. The man had a young son by the name of Bernardo or Bernard, who was between ten and fifteen years of age. Bernard was left alone when his father entered into the service of his country. Reportedly, he accidentally ingested some weed killer and died in the entranceway to the gatehouse. People have reported seeing the figure of a young man leaning against the wall of the building. He is bent over as if he is being sick to his stomach. Then he vanishes from sight.

Throughout the years the Adamson family had many animals, including cats, dogs, and horses. Their fondness toward their animals was illustrated by the numerous gravestones that were scattered throughout the property to mark the burial places of all their cherished pets. The stone markers were eventually gathered up and placed in one central location, near the main house.

The Adamson Estate has a resident dog named Zeph. The problem is that Zeph died in 1953, as testified by his tombstone in the pet cemetery. Zeph was Anthony's favourite dog. He would bound around the property and then come to a stop on his mat by the front door, where he would deposit his favourite stuffed toy. Zeph still seems to be running around the grounds, and occasionally leaves his stuffed toy just inside the front door. After Zeph's passing Anthony would discover the toy by the door and take it outside to Zeph's grave, by the north door of the building. Before Anthony knew it the toy would be back in the house.

I got in touch with clairvoyant John Carlos Perrone. I was intrigued to discover if my own intuition was right about the Adamson estate. Was Mabel still there? Was anyone else there?

John had visited the Adamson Estate a few months prior to my call. At the time he had no previous knowledge of the history of the Cawthra-Adamson family at Grove Farm. This is what he observed: "All the spirit energy is on the right side of the house. I can see a car arriving and a casket being carried into the house. The casket is placed in the large room situated on the first floor at the far right side of the building.

"I see a woman. She is sitting on a chair in the corner of the room. She is in mourning. They are holding a service for this deceased male. There is another death here. It is one of her sons. I think he died violently. I sense he was struck by a train. This occurred in the 1950s. There is not much left of the body. Maybe it was a plane crash. I can still see her.

"There is someone here who had a drinking problem. They worked here. He attempted suicide on two occasions, once in the water and once at the gatehouse. I see that he hung himself in the basement of the house. This is where he would go to drink. He was in his mid-forties. He is no longer here.

"I can tell the woman in mourning loves the fact that there are children in the house. Nevertheless, she is very depressed. Her time is spent reliving the loss of her husband and son. Occasionally the son visits her.

"I hear banging and things being thrown around. There is someone walking about."

Mabel Adamson was, by all accounts, a free spirit. Despite her attempts to live that way she suffered the great trauma of separation by war, and life after the war with a very changed husband. The estate seemed to be her only hope for happiness, but that too failed. Then her estranged husband died and a decade later she was crippled. Perhaps she still seeks some respite on her estate, perhaps her free spirit is determined to stay, by choice. Could Rodney be the other death? No doubt!

As for a suicide, there is no account of a man in his forties who worked on the grounds and took his life in the basement of the house, but there were many years relatively unaccounted for when the family was in England.

There was another rather eerie presence that John encountered on the property — coming from the lake itself. "There is energy coming off the water. I see soldiers being transported in a small supply ship. This event is happening during the War of 1812. The ship is now sinking. The entire crew has drowned." John indicated that at night these lost souls come to shore. What are they searching for? According to John, they reach the Adamson house but cannot enter. They peer in at the windows. The proof of their existence is fingerprints on the window panes of the house in the morning. This has been partially confirmed by the cleaning staff, who regularly complain of fingerprints on the windows when they arrive in the morning.

A naval historian in the area has no record of a supply ship sinking near the Adamson property during the War of 1812, but that does not necessarily exclude the possibility. It would explain the inability of the spirits to enter the house, since it was erected fifty years after their death!

Now that the Adamson house is home to the Royal Conservatory of Music, students of all ages arrive daily to study their particular musical instrument. I spoke with Stephen Greene, associate dean of the school. I asked him if he or his staff had ever experienced any ghostly activity in the building. He had a couple of good stories indicating some evidence of paranormal activity. Stephen told me about the time they had set the chairs up in the far right side room on the first floor of the house for a performance that was happening the next day. (This is the same room where John saw the apparition of a woman in mourning.) The next day the staff arrived and discovered that all the chairs had been moved away. The motion detector goes off in the middle of the night for no apparent reason. One time all the faculty mugs simply vanished from the main-floor staff kitchen, never to be seen again. Stephen also confirmed the cleaning staff complaints about finger smudges on the windows.

When I entered the Adamson house I experienced a wave of disappointment. There was little evidence that the Adamson family had ever occupied this space. A glance up the central staircase did reveal two stained-glass window panes showing the Adamson family crests. I mused about the original interior of this home: what about the fashionable carpets and the needlepoint-upholstered furniture? What ever happened to the mummy's hand? What had become of their former servant staff of four?

Despite the lack of historical evidence in the form of Adamson artifacts, there was still the feeling of strong spirit presence in the building and the surrounding grounds.

In houses that have been altered, spirits often walk on original stairs and where ceilings and floors have been changed they appear half on one floor and half on another. Maybe in their dimension they can still see furniture that is no longer present in this dimension. For them the mummy's hand could still be in the attic, and the groundskeeper's son is being sick in the archway. The windows could be as walls to the spirits from the water, and Zeph could still be playing in the yard. Just because we do not see, does not mean it cannot be!

Old Barber House Restaurant

~ Streetsville ~

Who are these strangers in my tranquil abode, who appear and then vaporize in the darkness? Could they be hallucinations? How is it possible for people from the twenty-first century to encounter characters from the nineteenth century under one roof at one time?

This experience could be yours if you visit the Barber House Restaurant in Streetsville, Ontario. This restaurant was once the home of William Barber, an acclaimed textile manufacturer from Georgetown, who established a small community named Barbertown with his brothers, around their mill site just south of Streetsville.

The 1877 Pope Atlas of Peel County described this successful Barber family operation. In 1843 the Barber Brothers and Mr. B. Franklin (a brother-in-law) started a woollen mill in Streetsville, of about the same proportions as the one already in existence at Georgetown. As the area grew so did each factory, until the Georgetown mill had more machinery than it had power to run and the one in Streetsville had more machinery than buildings. A new building was planned and erected at the Streetsville location in 1852, and the machinery from both mills was installed there, creating one of the most extensive textile manufacturers in Ontario. Total factory costs were in the range of $200,000 and it employed between 150 and 200 workers. In 1861 the mill was destroyed by fire and an even larger factory was built.

During that period there was also a sawmill, a machine shop, a blacksmith shop, and a carpenter's shop within the factory complex, which was built on the banks of the Credit River and designed with the workers' health in mind. It was almost like a village, with residences of the proprietors alongside the works, forty-three dwellings in all, built for the comfort and convenience of the workers. This mill complex, known as the Toronto Woollen Mills, was the fourth-largest textile mill in Ontario.

In the early days William Barber and his wife, Mary, chose to live in Georgetown. In the late 1850s Mary died in childbirth, leaving him with their three-year-old son, Robert. In 1860 William married Elizabeth Webster, a woman only sixteen years of age; William was a youthful forty-eight. Mary Finley, a direct descendant of William Barber, believes that prior to the marriage, Elizabeth may have been young Robert's nanny.

William decided to make a fresh start in Streetsville. He built a matrimonial home for his young wife on a site just up the road from Barbertown. Construction of the two-storey Victorian mansion began in 1861 and was completed a year later. The Barbers and Elizabeth's brother and his family made it their home.

William had certainly wanted to ensure Elizabeth's happiness. The house he built suited both their business needs and their social position. Four fireplaces with marble mantelpieces warmed the front parlour, the dining room, and two upstairs bedrooms. It was a centre-hall plan with an exquisite, curved staircase winding to the second floor.

Imagine how awe inspiring it must have been for the then eighteen-year-old wife to occupy such a grand residence. What a place to begin their journey together, and for Elizabeth to give birth to four children.

Unfortunately, tragedy soon struck in the form of a cholera epidemic. The Barbers' three-and-a-half-year-old daughter, Louisa, was struck with the illness and died. According to Mrs. Finley, "The medical officer of health at the time informed William that the cholera germs could still be present in his library books. He advised William to burn every book in his library, including the family bible. William was beset with remorse and had one of his own employees conduct the deed. That employee was later gifted a sideboard for his troubles."

The syndicate of William Barber and Brothers owned everything in common, without any deed of partnership or any division of profits, with each owner drawing according to his requirements.

Joseph Barber Jr. and Bennet Franklin retired in 1869, and James took over the Georgetown mill, which he continued to run with his three sons. William and Robert carried on the woollen operation. The Toronto Woollen Mills flourished for another decade, but by the 1880s a trend toward cotton caused the business to falter. The mill went into receivership in 1882, and the Canadian Bank of Commerce took over the property. This did not mean that William Barber was bankrupt. His other holdings allowed him to continue his current lifestyle. According to Mrs. Finley, William Barber was heartbroken over losing the mill.

Other companies attempted to make a go of the textile operation, but never succeeded. The community of Barberton had always relied on the profitability of the mill to survive. Today, without reading the plaques on the site, no one would ever believe that a thriving community of homes and stores once existed here.

William passed away in 1889. Elizabeth, for unknown reasons, sold their matrimonial home shortly thereafter and relocated to Toronto. The Barber legacy had come to an end in Streetsville.

Since then, a number of families have occupied the former Barber estate. In 1981, Carol and Jerry Townsend sold the home to Tome Petrovski, whose dream was to turn the house into a fine-dining establishment. However, for a period of time the house stood vacant. Vandals broke in one night, stole the marble fireplace mantles on the first floor of the building, and set fire to the premises. Neighbours spotted smoke billowing out of the structure and alerted the fire department. Fortunately, the firefighters were able to save the historic home.

Mr. Tome Petrovski invested a considerable amount of time and money into the restoration of and renovations to the Barber House. He finally opened the restaurant 1984. Today, his son Victor manages the daily operations and oversees the wedding receptions on site. Tome is still involved with the business. Their menu statement best sums up their operations: "Enjoy continental cuisine that will gratify the most discerning palate."

But is the Barber House Restaurant haunted? Yes it is!

However, the spirit activity here presents itself in a very different fashion from the usual haunting. This site is a prime example of inter-dimensional time travel, or the overlapping of dimensions, involving more than one century of activity. The Barber family from the 1860s still inhabit their residence, as well as Victor Petrovski, his staff, and the diners of the Barber House Restaurant.

The Barber House represents a sample of how we see ourselves in time. Maurice Nicoll writes *In Psychological Commentaries on the Teachings of Gurdjieff and Ouspentsy,* "We do not see the Time-Bodies of ourselves or of things. We think the past is dead. Our lives are living lines in living Time. Owing to our relationship to Time, however, we see only a point in Time and then another and we call them present moments."

I met Mary Finley at the Barber House Restaurant for a tour of the premises. Mary is an extraordinary person, who works tirelessly as a volunteer and historical advocate throughout the city of Mississauga. Mary is also convinced that her forefathers are still living in their former home ... or is it their present home?

When you meet Mary, and listen to her stories about the Barber family, you sense she is with them. In fact, I kept looking around to see if any of the Barbers of the 1860s had joined us. Mary knows the characters as well as if she had lived with them.

There is another Barber descendant who shares the same views: Mary's sister, Phyllis Barber.

Mary toured me through the building and provided me with a good overview of how the Barber family used each room. At one point, Victor (the manager) joined us in the hallway near the front door. I asked him if he had ever experienced any unexplained activity in the house. When he said "No," I decided to give him some examples.

"For instance, you think you saw a figure go into a room, but upon investigating find the room empty. You might feel a cold spot in the building or notice that some silverware has disappeared from a dining table."

He looked at me and replied, "Well there was this experience I had near Christmas last year. I was standing right here in the hallway, in front of the wine cabinet at your left as you enter the building. We had a number of Christmas cards standing on the shelf of the wine cabinet. Suddenly this little breeze of air came by in the hallway and one Christmas card began to spin round and round, but never fell off the shelf. I just stood there and watched it."

Mary commented, "Where the wine cabinet is now was originally the doorway into the front room."

Was it possible that this slight breeze could have been someone coming or going through this original doorway?

Shortly after that, Mary took me upstairs to show me where there had once been a secret room in the house. She led me to a small room to the right of the staircase landing. At one time this space served as a small back bedroom. Although everything has been altered as a result of renovations, Mary explained what had been there when she was in the building prior to its sale in 1981. "You would enter the closet and take two steps, then turn sideways and take three steps to your right. Then you came upon a secret entranceway that led into a small room, in which you could just stand up. I believe this secret room was built by William Barber in order to hide former slaves en route via the Underground Railroad."

Was this possible?

I spoke with Karolyn Smardz Frost, who has an infinite knowledge of Canadian history, archaeology, and heritage education. Karolyn is well versed in the subject of the Underground Railroad, a secret operation carried out by courageous people to free slaves.

Did we still have safe houses for former slaves in Ontario during the 1860s? Her answer was no. By 1860 there was no longer any need for such hideaways when we already had established black settlements in the country. There was no need for them to hide. Perhaps William Barber felt otherwise. We may never know what the reason was for there being a secret room in the house.

Although Mary has never actually seen her deceased relations, her sister has.

One time the two women were climbing the stairs when Phyllis saw a female spirit. She explains, "I saw this woman coming down the stairs. I knew she was someone from the past. She was wearing a standard fitted bodice and skirt with a shawl draped over her shoulders. She was not young. I would say middle-aged. I felt her skirt brush by me as she continued her descent.

"There is another woman I have seen standing on the second floor balcony at the front of the house. She is staring out over the grounds. She looks quite forlorn, as if she's anxious or upset about something. She must have lived here in the house."

I wondered if one of these women could be Elizabeth Barber; I also wondered who else Phyllis has seen. She continues, "The Victorian room on the second floor is, to my eyes, a nursery. I see a crib, rocking horses, and tin soldiers. I see a doll sitting in the corner of the room.

"I get the feeling the room is waiting for someone — for a child to come back."

I asked her how clearly she could see these deceased people and events.

"I see things just as clearly as if I was looking at a photograph."

It is this ability that Phyllis has to "see" that confirms that the Barber family are still in the house. Her ability to observe detail is amazing.

Phyllis highlighted an event she witnessed from another time period. "I have seen people from the past dining in the room to the right as you enter the house. The table was set with candles and flowers. There was a formal dinner going on. I could see many diners and one woman with a rose in her hair.

"Then I saw some men gathered by the fireplace. They had drinks in their hands and were smoking.

"There was a bowl of roses and good crystal and linen on a table in the room."

On one occasion Phyllis was seated in the Green Room of the present-day restaurant, by the fireplace, having dinner. The room was full of diners. Then: "There was a floral arrangement on the mantelpiece. Everyone in the room was seated at the time. Suddenly the floral arrangement flew off the mantelpiece and crashed onto the floor. The room went silent. Everyone just looked amazed over this unexplained event."

A few years ago the Petrovskis had an addition built onto the house, to serve as a dining/reception room for banquets and weddings. Phyllis is not happy about this space. During one visit she realized the reason why. "As I entered the doorway to this room I didn't like the feeling. I sensed someone was really upset. I had to force myself to sit down with Mary to eat. Someone was very upset, angry, and agitated and I asked Mary if we could move.

"Then I saw him. He was fairly short, with wavy hair. He was wearing a pinstriped suit and carrying a pocket watch. I recognized the timepiece as a Barber heirloom. He was pacing back and forth, back and forth. Then I recognized him to be William Barber. I knew instantly that he was distressed because the addition had been built over his garden."

Later she saw William again. This time he was walking the grounds with his pet dog — a Jack Russell. On one occasion he was smoking a pipe, and on another a cigar.

On another visit she encountered the woman on the stairs again. This time Phyllis felt that "she was looking right at us."

I returned to the Barber Restaurant to interview Victor Petrovski. Although he had stated earlier that he hadn't really encountered any paranormal activity until he realized the significance of the incident with the Christmas card, I was hoping to get more stories. I probed to see how he really felt about spirit activity and if he was a believer.

"I want to believe in it, and sometimes I do — sometimes I don't," he admitted. "Most of the time things happen about mid-afternoon when there are no customers. I might catch a movement. I think I see someone walk into a dining room. I follow them into the room, but there is no one there and there is no exit … I don't actually see a person, but my mind is saying someone just walked into the room.

"My cousin sees spirits. He says he has seen a little girl on the staircase.

"Upstairs some of the windows are actually closed off. They are covered over. In the covered-over windows in the men's room my cousin has seen faces of people. He senses that they are happy. They enjoy being able to move around freely."

"What about Phyllis's lady on the stairs?" I asked.

"We once had a dishwasher who was quite a religious fellow. He was in his sixties. He would come to me and say, 'The lady came into the kitchen.' He told me she was a young woman dressed in white and black. He saw her on several occasions.

"One Christmas one waiter saw the little girl running on the stairs.

"There was a fellow here in the mid-1980s who would say he could sense someone around him."

The men's washroom on the second floor also seems to be an active area. Victor shared another incident. "I once owned a restaurant out at the Toronto Airport. I had a regular customer there who had no idea that I was involved in the Barber Restaurant in Streetsville. He was there for dinner and had gone upstairs to use the washroom. As he entered the room he saw a ghost and fled. When he returned to his table his wife said he looked as white as a sheet.

"Another time a man dining in the restaurant told me he was a psychic. He indicated that someone didn't want him there."

Wanted or not wanted, past or present, real or unreal, the Barber Restaurant has many guests. Inevitably many old mansions are destined to become public places of some kind, and we get to enjoy their history, not to mention their mystery, and their living past.

Why did the Barbers need a secret room? Who is the little girl? Why did Elizabeth sell the house? Is William really upset with the changes? Does he think it is still his home? What is the connection that Mary and Phyllis have now with their ancestors, with their heritage? Who wanted the psychic to leave, and why?

Many seemingly unrelated events, many unanswered questions, many opportunities to experience the overlays of time.

Go out for dinner. Have a good "time"! Share in the "activity"!

Oakville Museum/ Erchless Estate

~ Oakville ~

Have you ever visited a museum and felt someone watching you when no one was there? Can you recall a time when you were alone but heard whispers? Have you ever wished you could step back in time, or yearn to have these experiences? If so, you might want to visit the Oakville Museum of History at the Erchless Estate. Where history comes alive, in more ways than one.

Many museums in Canada are associated with some form of paranormal activity in connection with an artifact in their collection, or due to the historical significance of the site or the buildings. Erchless Estate, now the Oakville Museum of History, is no different. In fact, it is home to at least seven spirits!

The story of the estate begins with the founder of Oakville, Colonel William Chisholm. Nick and Helma Mika wrote, in their book entitled *Places in Ontario*, "William Chisholm had moved with his Loyalist family to the Burlington Beach area in 1793. In 1816, William Chisholm settled in Nelson Township and became a successful storekeeper, timber merchant and ship owner. In 1827, he purchased 960 acres at the mouth

Erchless Estate, on the left. The former Custom House and bank are on the right side.

The magnificent view from the Erchless Estate of Lake Ontario and the harbour.

of Sixteen Mile Creek during a public auction and on that site he built mills, laid out a town plot, and opened the harbour for shipping." The site had once been the Mississauga Indian reserve.

The meaning of the word Mississauga is "people who live where there are many rivers." The Mississaugas belonged to the Ojibwa First Nation, who called Sixteen Mile Creek Nanzuhzaugewazog, meaning "having two outlets," because of the gravel bar dividing the mouth of the creek.

In 1834, Colonel Chisholm was appointed collector of customs for the port, and the following year he became the postmaster.

By 1839, Chisholm moved to the foot of Navy Street by the harbour. The Mikas add, "Recognizing that waterpower was essential for industrial growth, Chisholm formed the Oakville Hydraulic Company which was financed by a number of inhabitants. The venture proved to be an impractical project and the business failed." Those who had invested money lost heavily. Colonel Chisholm died shortly after the matter was disclosed, at the age of fifty-four.

One of the bedrooms on the second floor decorated as it would have appeared in the 1920s.

William's son, Robert Kerr Chisholm, built the Custom House in the harbour in 1856, as an office for custom services. The Bank of Toronto occupied one room of the building and the bank manager lived upstairs. Today the structure is attached to the Erchless Estate and holds museum exhibits.

In 1858, Robert Chisholm completed the construction of his own home, next to the Custom House. This Italianate-style residence still stands, on a knoll overlooking the picturesque harbour. He named his home Erchless, a Gaelic word representing the clan seat and castle of the Chisholm's of Inverness-Shire, Scotland. Robert's son, Allan Chisholm, subsequently inherited the estate.

By 1920 some of the smaller bedrooms had been converted to bathrooms. At this time Emelda, the widow of John Alexander Chisholm, moved into the home with her two daughters, Hazel and Juliet. Further changes were made to the home. Emelda died at Erchless in 1951. Her daughter Hazel founded the Oakville Historical Society just one year later.

In the early eighties, after six generations of Chisholms, the town of Oakville bought Erchless with plans to convert it into the present-day museum. In the early stages of the project, the rooms in the house were rented out as apartments for six years. No one knew until later that the house was still occupied by its former residents. Rebecca and Emelda Chisholm are still there, as are a cook, two children, and one other unidentified individual. Even the Chisholm's butler, Christopher Columbus Lee, an African American, is still there.

As early at the 1830s, the town of Oakville was a gateway to Canada for many African Americans escaping American slavery. Oakville was part of the Underground Railroad. Ships from Oakville sailed throughout the Great Lakes and beyond, and many slaves were stowed away in grain vessels. There are stories of a tunnel that ran from the Sixteen Mile Creek to the Herb Merry House, on Trafalgar Road. There is also some evidence to suggest there may have been a tunnel leading under Navy Street from somewhere near to the Custom House.

The Underground Railroad doubled Ontario's African-American population, from about 20,000 to 40,000, in the first ten years after the Americans passed the Fugitive Slave Act in 1850. The act encouraged the capture and return to slavery of African Americans.

Wendy Belcher, member of the Oakville Historical Society and ghost walk tour guide.

I travelled to Oakville in the fall of 2014 to meet Wendy Belcher, a retired school teacher and active member of the Oakville Historical Society. Wendy agreed to meet with me and discuss the history of the Chisholms and the haunting of Erchless. She is very familiar with the ghost stories associated with the house and grounds because she is one of the guides for the popular ghost-walk tours of the historic district of Oakville. The tours run each year from mid-October through to October 29th. Wendy informed me, "For the past three years we have had a total of two thousand people on our ghost tours."

When you first see Erchless you cannot help being struck with the beautiful, natural setting of this four-acre estate. The home, as well as the Custom House, look out over the majestic harbour. The Erchless Estate gardens have been carefully restored to their historic appearance, from photographs taken in the early 1900s.

Wendy and I sat at a picnic table on the grounds to begin our discussion of the spirits of Erchless. Wendy began, "Sometimes in the morning you will hear children running up the stairs of the museum as if they are trying to hide. Staff also hear the children whispering, 'They're coming, they're coming.'" One museum worker said that when it's her turn to open the building she often hears a child running away and giggling. Her impression is of a happy little girl, who seems to be playing a game. It was noted that Hazel and her sister, Juliet, had played in the house as children. They moved into the home with their mother Emelda in 1920.

Wendy also talked about when Erchless was a rooming house. It seems inconceivable now that such a stately home could ever have become a rooming house. During our discussion, Wendy mentioned the sighting of a spirit near a flower garden on the property. Sometime later I discovered two small paper booklets being sold at the Historical Society office, entitled *Ghosts of Oakville*, 1999, and *Boo Too Ghosts of Oakville and Halton*, 2003. The books were researched by Joyce Burnell, a friend of the Oakville Historical Society who has since passed on. I found the reference to the garden spirit in Joyce's first booklet in a story entitled "The Flower Lady."

Joyce had interviewed a female tenant who lived at Erchless during the rooming-house days. The woman had a remarkable experience.

We lived in the main house in a front apartment overlooking Lake Ontario and the mouth of the Sixteen Mile Creek. I loved gardening. There was an area near the front door which had a foot-high box-hedge perimeter that we called the maze. I'm sorry to say this it has now been removed. In this area I planted some vegetables. One day while I was cultivating my yellow beans I sensed someone behind me. Turning around I saw a woman in the flower garden beside the wrought-iron fence. She was just standing there with a big basket in her hand, as if collecting flowers. Her dark hair was very severely pulled back. She wore a light-coloured dress with some kind of design like bows or flowers on the skirt. I stared at her and she stared at me. Then she disappeared in front of my eyes. For a moment or two I wondered if I had gone nuts.

The iron gate and fence where a former tenant saw the spirit of a woman picking flowers in the garden.

This is quite an amazing encounter. She actually witnessed a full apparition of a woman picking flowers, right down to the details of her dress. The most moving part is the acknowledgement of one another through eye contact. Could this spirit perhaps have just been in her own time frame and the tenant glimpsed the past? Or was this occurrence happening in the present?

The tenant was shocked, but curious about the experience. She went to the Custom House next door, where the museum was at the time. Interested to learn more about the original owners of Erchless, she asked museum staff if they had any photographs of the Chisholms. They showed her a picture of Rebecca, wife of William Chisholm. According to the tenant, the picture of Rebecca looked amazingly similar to the flower lady she had seen in the garden.

Wendy then told the story of another sighting, this time inside the building. "The museum is closed to the public on Mondays. Staff members work on those days. It was during a Monday meeting that members of the staff witnessed a mysterious figure who passed by the open door and then walked through a wall and vanished."

Joyce Burnell described the figure: "It was definitely a dark, male figure, wearing a long black coat, just like the ghost seen at another time by a painter working in the building."

Wendy commented, "Staff then asked, 'Who was that?' Nobody had an answer."

One female museum employee, identified as Carol (an alias), who had worked at the museum for fourteen years prior to 1999, relayed to Joyce a fascinating experience she had had in the education room in the museum. This was Emelda's bedroom.

"This is the oldest part of the building. It is a beautiful well-lit room, serene and peaceful. There is a sample of Emelda's wallpaper still on the wall. Sometimes I used to get away from office interruptions by going to this lovely room to work. I would be working away until about mid-afternoon — it mostly happened then. I would get a foreboding feeling; there would suddenly seem to be a presence behind me. I would turn around and there would be no one there. I had to get out of that room. It was eerie.

"There was also a student who once experienced something in that room. She was there working on a slide presentation. The time was also mid-afternoon when she couldn't stay there any longer. She felt a very heavy, depressing, sad feeling."

Upon reading this passage, I wondered what had happened in that room to leave such an energy imprint of depression, sadness, or foreboding.

Wendy told me about another experience that related specifically to Emelda. "Staff were rearranging the furniture in Emelda's former sitting room. They wanted to create a study area. Once the room had been changed, the staff experienced a cold and uninviting atmosphere. The museum called in a medium, who instructed staff to put the furniture back where it had been before. As soon as they had done this everything settled down."

Joyce Burnell wrote about another unexplained event with a handyman. He had also seen the black figure that staff had witnessed during a meeting. "We had a handyman who worked evenings. He painted, did some carpentry. One evening he was painting the upstairs education room. He was alone when he heard people talking and loud footsteps coming up the stairs. Thinking some of the staff had come back for something, he waited. Nobody appeared and he went out to see who was there. Seeing no one, he returned to his painting.

The window on the left is where a visitor saw a woman wearing a black dress.

"Sometime later, he heard footsteps again on the stairs. This time he went quickly to see who was there. Just as he reached the landing and peered through the railing he saw a black figure turning the corner at the end of the stairs, moving along the hallway. He called out but received no answer. He felt too uncomfortable to stay around any longer and left in a hurry. He felt he was being warned to get out of the room." Could this have been Christopher Columbus Lee, the butler?

Carol also shared a story with Joyce about the alarm system in the building. "We have a rather complicated alarm system in the building, which has to be turned off when anyone enters. I came to work one morning around eight-fifteen a.m., and when I opened the door I found all the lights were flashing and switching, going crazy. I immediately got through to the alarm company and they didn't have a record of activity going on in the building. When I walked away from the main door and through the lobby, suddenly a lightshade fell from the ceiling and missed me by inches. On my way upstairs I could hear office noises. In the office I found all the machines going crazy. Our fax machines were all ringing, our photocopier was spewing out papers, the typewriter was turned on and was tapping away on its own. I was terrified and made a quick exit down the stairs. By the time I had reached the bottom, I realized that things were silent again upstairs. I went back up and everything seemed normal.

"The alarm company had no explanation for what had taken place, and neither did I."

Wendy mentioned the existence of a photograph of a female looking out the upstairs window on the west end of the house. "In the upper left window is a figure of a woman pulling the drapes back to look out. At the time there was no one in the museum."

Wendy talked about uninvited guests. The grounds of Erchless are quite picturesque and attract bridal parties having their pictures taken. Wendy tells me, "One party had their pictures developed and discovered an additional person in the wedding photograph that was not present at the wedding."

She highlighted another odd experience. "In 2006, six people were standing on the sidewalk in front of the house. Suddenly a flash occurred from inside the museum. I thought they were taking pictures, but no one had a camera. I checked with the town but there was no one in the building at the time."

The downstairs room in the Custom Building is another area exhibiting paranormal activity. The upstairs room of the structure is office space for museum staff. The Customs Building was where people who immigrated by boat had to report upon arriving in the harbour. According to museum staff, some people were quarantined here as a result of disease. Eventually, after treatment, they would be allowed into the community. Museum staff on occasion will hear whispers. They are unable to tell if the whispers are male or female voices and they seem to be throughout the room.

In "The Flower Lady," Joyce ends with the strongest incident experienced by the female tenant she interviewed. "One night when I was alone, reading in bed, I felt a weight on the bed beside me, as if someone was getting into the bed. Shocked, I looked up quickly but there was nobody there, only an imprint on the bed cover. Then I felt a hand touch my bare arm and move slowly along it. The hairs progressively stood up on that arm giving me a weird feeling. It was incredibly strange but not really frightening. I could say that, in my six years of living at Erchless, I knew our ghost meant no harm."

After my interview with Wendy, I entered Erchless to tour the museum. Would I see anything or sense a presence? One never knows when such a thing will happen. When it does it is always a surprise. A young woman greeted me at the reception desk. I told her why I was there. Had she ever had a paranormal experience in the museum, I asked. The answer was no!

She explained to me that I could tour the oldest section of the house where the historical exhibits were on display, but I could not enter the living quarters that the Chisholms had shared until the guide arrived to conduct the tour.

In the original, old, section of house, I toured the kitchen, hoping to catch a glimpse of the cook or the butler, Christopher Columbus Lee. There was nothing, no feeling of a presence. I continued on my tour. It was fascinating to view the old section of the building, but I couldn't wait to tour the parlour and bedrooms that the Chisholms once occupied. I had been told that this section of the house had been restored to its former elegance of 1925.

The tour guide arrived and I joined a small group as they entered this part of the house. The downstairs, including a dining room and parlour, is very elegant and stately. A sweeping staircase leads to the grand upstairs bedrooms. All the rooms in the house contain memorabilia of the Chisholm family. You can really sense what it must have been like to live in this setting. However, at no time did I feel a presence or see anything unusual. I took several pictures, but only my own appreciation developed.

There is no question that Erchless is a setting worth visiting. Visitors and museum staff have had some extraordinary experiences. Erchless is a timeless place waiting for the right people to truly witness the past and present in real time.

Beild House Country Inn and Spa

~ Collingwood ~

Upon checking in, blood pressure 151/87. Upon checking out, blood pressure 122/68. That says it all. When it is dinnertime the Barefoot Contessa arrives at the table. All is well at the Beild Country Inn and Spa, where you get so much more than a good night's sleep!

The history of the Beild House dates back to 1909, when Dr. Joseph Robbins Arthur chose Eden Smith, an architect of choice for Toronto's wealthy class, to design a residence cum office for him on Hurontario Street in Collingwood, Ontario.

Smith was English born and had been acclaimed for single-handedly revolutionizing domestic architecture in Canada. He disliked the massive arches, ostentatious towers, and fussy Victorian verandahs that characterized most of the large houses under construction at the turn of the century. His pared-down designs, stripped of any extraneous ornamentation, reflected his fondness for the comfortable country cottages of the old country, and become known as the English Cottage style. This style of design offered steeply pitched roofs, tall chimneys, and rows of casement windows.

The Beild Country Inn and Spa as it appears today.

Construction of the home began in 1909. No one, however, could have imagined the challenges that would soon be faced. Dr. Arthur's daughter, Bethia, who was seven when they moved into the house, explained that it took three years to build the structure. Builders unexpectedly encountered a layer of limestone bedrock. The rock had to be blasted to make trenches for the water pipes.

Smith erected an unusual-looking red-brick and shingle-sided structure, supported by massive steel beams. The doctor's consulting rooms and offices were relegated to the colder and noisier north end of the building. The living and dining rooms were trimmed in gumwood and warmed by simple but elegant back-to-back fireplaces. They faced south, toward the garden. The spacious attic became a billiard room and the children's playroom. Bethia and her younger brother and friends spent many happy hours playing there on a set of gymnastic rings. Bethia recalled, "Anyone who could swing high enough would write their initials on the ceiling." The home boasted 9,700 square feet of living space, including a gorgeous carriage house still on the property today.

Dr. Arthur was a well-respected physician, who practised into his eighties. He also served as mayor of Collingwood in 1919 and again from 1923 to 1929. His wife, Katherine, was a commissioner of the Girl Guides and regent of the Imperial Order of the Daughter's of the Empire (IODE). Today the IODE is known as a Canadian women's volunteer organization.

Katherine's sister, Margaret Rose, was one of the first women to earn a master's degree from the University of Toronto. Their father, Henry Robinson, was a pioneer lawyer who played an active role in the development of Collingwood. Robinson came to live at Beild House with his daughter after he spent his considerable wealth on an extravagant trip around the world. He truly believed he was destined to die in his sixtieth year, and the trip was his swan song. To his disappointment, he lived to be eighty-two.

During the depression, transients who passed through the community could be sure of a hot meal and clean clothing at Dr. Arthur's office. It also became a place of refuge for women widowed during the First World War, who were forced to take their children and leave their homes to find shelter since they were not permitted to inherit and run a home on their own. It was a time of old-fashioned attitudes. In fact, the era was tightly gripped by strong Victorian beliefs. To this day the inn still represents this time period with presentation and in personal service.

Dr. Arthur and his wife, Katherine, followed the precepts of the Victorian era. The couple resided on the second floor of the house. Katherine had her bedroom at one end of the hall and her husband at the other end. During construction of the building he had a secret passageway built to link those bedrooms, as it was considered unbecoming for servants to witness the husband entering his wife's bedroom or to be seen departing later. It was all very hush, hush! The Arthurs raised five children, nonetheless.

When Bethia was a young child she contracted tuberculosis. She was moved to what is now room 5, which had been her father's smoking lounge. He treated her ailment by designing a bed that could be swung out to a second-floor porch accessible from the room so that Bethia could breathe the fresh air. It was common practice to place patients on verandahs where they could breathe clean, cold air for a few hours a day. Doctors believed fresh air was the best treatment for lung diseases.

Bethia overcame the illness and went on to live a full life, later operating the home as a shelter for the needy. In her old age, Bethia sold the family home to the Kentucky Fried Chicken head office. That company converted the house into offices and a teaching space. New owners of Kentucky Fried Chicken franchises were trained here, and learned the secret recipes. When the company sold the estate they left with some of the personal furnishings once owned by the Arthur family.

At this point in time the Beild house was silent. Concerned characters from the past were awaiting the return to good hospitality and personal service. It had been some time since they had felt true companionship and caring of the spirit. They were watching the barefoot contessa and her handsome gentleman — they were watching Stephanie.

Stephanie met her future husband in a grocery store. His name was Bill Christie Barclay. His great-great-grandfather was William Mellis Christie, founder of the original Mr. Christie's Bakery Company.

When Bill Christie Barclay met Stephanie he was the night manager at The Kitchen Table at Yonge and St. Clair Avenue. The two of them would meet for a coffee at Fran's. Eventually they married.

Unbeknownst to them, Beild House was waiting! Stephanie told me that "Bill wanted to own and operate a bed and breakfast."

In 1981, Stephanie and Bill discovered Collingwood, and Beild House. There was something very familiar about the house to both of them. The couple bought the house and soon opened the Beild House Country Inn and Spa, Collingwood's best-kept secret.

By 2014, Stephanie and Bill had operated the establishment for thirty-three years. Unfortunately, Bill passed away that year, leaving Stephanie saddened and introspective about her life, but still a vibrant and caring owner.

In September 2014 I phoned the Beild Inn to inquire if I could put their story in a book. Stephanie answered the phone. I explained who I was, and my reason for the call. Stephanie was pleased to respond with an invitation to experience the energy there. "You need to come and stay here. I will arrange everything." I thanked her and we set a date. My interest was piqued and Stephanie was anxious to share.

She stated, "I can 'hear' my guests. If you can understand voice tone you will discover the combination of needs and the person's outlook. From this, I will be able to cater to their specific needs. People like a little intrigue. Travelling is such a personal experience."

The former bed of King Edward VIII, in room 4.

When I had set the date to arrive, Stephanie asked me which room I wanted to stay in. It was either room 4 or 5. She explained if I were to choose room 4, I would have the opportunity to sleep in the former bed of King Edward VIII. I thought to myself, *how did she ever end up owning this bed?* Edward VIII was the king who had abdicated the throne on December 11, 1936, to become engaged to American socialite Wallis Simpson, who was seeking a divorce from her second husband. That couple was wed in France on June 3, 1937, settling first in Florida, United States, and later returning to France where they stayed for the remainder of their lives.

I chose room 4. My wife and I arrived two weeks later. Did the spirits of Beild House know we were coming?

The moment we stepped inside the Beild Country Inn and Spa we received a friendly welcome and were escorted to our room. Staff informed us that Stephanie was out, but would return shortly to greet us. As we entered the room we couldn't help but be drawn to the royal bed. This was the bed of the former King of England and his wife, the Duchess of

The portrait of William Christie hanging over the fireplace.

Windsor. Photographs of the royal family adorned one wall, as well as a gas fireplace. The bed had been slightly redesigned to accommodate a queen size. It had been beautifully done, in keeping with its original design.

We returned to the first floor and toured the dining room, the living room, and a cozy sitting room. There is a small space next to the dining room with some reading material, dvds to take back to your room, and beverages. One wall in this space is decorated with photographs of the families of Bill and Stephanie.

Over the fireplace in the dining room there is a portrait of Bill's great-great-grandfather, William Christie. A chair is set nearby. This chair was once owned by Mary Jane, William Christie's wife.

Stephanie arrived and we did the introductions. She is a very strong woman, with determination and a zest for life. Her aim is to make her guests' stay a memorable experience. She explained about the spirit activity in the home. She talked about Dr. Arthur's comings and goings. He wears a top hat and tails, his preferred attire when officiating as mayor

The chair once owned by Mary Jane Christie. Her presence is still felt when you sit in the chair.

(Below) The elaborate setting of the living room, with a large collection of porcupine-quill boxes under the glass on the coffee table.

or attending a dinner party. The doctor has been seen walking downstairs to the lower level of the building, where he did surgery and dispensed his medicines. The doctor has also been sighted in room 4, walking up the stairs to the third floor where the children slept. It had been his habit to say goodnight to them there. Guests on the second floor have reported two women in the hallway, talking and laughing in the night.

The Beild Inn has also been featured on the television show *Rescue Mediums*, and the Cold Spot Paranormal Research Group has been there as well. Their investigations revealed that a "ghostly appearance of a man wearing a white tie and tails, top hat and cloak was seen standing in the archway. Then he backed away into the darkness."

Talking with employees brought them to the discovery of footsteps on the stairs and "unknown voices coming from the old doctor's examination room, as if patients were still waiting to be seen by the doctor."

As evening approached, Allanah (my wife) and I met two other guests staying at the inn for the week, Vijai and her niece Sharada. We were the only people booked in for that night.

Stephanie, seated to the left, and Allanah O'Boyle, discussing the history of the Beild Inn.

Vijai had just published a book titled *Re-Membering Your True Self*. Sharada had come from Toronto on business. Her aunt had come along to keep her company and to promote her book locally. Sharada spoke about how the house had been calling to her. She knew she was meant to stay there.

We sat down for a delicious dinner together and the four of us spent the evening conversing about spiritualism and related topics. It was such an amazing coincidence. I know Stephanie watched closely. This is part of the magic; the spiritual connection and the hospitality of the house. Stephanie is the producer and director of the spiritual connections.

After an evening stroll we all retired. Sharada and her aunt were staying in the three-room suite that had originally been Dr. Arthur's main-floor office. Sharada said she was nervous of seeing something and had decided to sleep with Vijai.

Allanah and I retired to room 4, and the king's bed. I had asked Stephanie how she came to possess this bed. She explained, "When the king abdicated and planned to leave the country, he had the opportunity to take any furniture he desired. He chose his bedroom suite, among other items...."

Allanah O'Boyle on the left, having a conversation about spiritualism with Vijai on the front right and Sharada.

Stephanie explained her connection: "My godmother was a singer and entertainer, working in Florida. She entertained Edward, then the Duke of Windsor, and Wallis…. My godmother was hired several times to entertain at their dinner parties. When the duke and duchess decided to move to France they didn't want to move everything. Since my godmother had been good to them, she was given the bedroom suite." Subsequently, it ended up in Stephanie's hands.

I asked Stephanie if her godmother was famous. She quickly confirmed that she was, but refused to name her — "all in good time."

I had no trouble falling into a deep sleep. Sometime in the night I was awakened by two women having a conversation in the hallway, just outside our door. Although I could hear them, I could not make out what they were saying. I thought it was rather impolite to have a conversation in the hallway in front of another guest's door in the middle of the night, and went back to sleep. I did not think of waking Allanah, nor did I investigate! In the morning I recalled the disturbance in the night, and thought it must have been guests who had arrived after we went to bed. But I also remembered the story of two female spirits talking in the night. Could that have been them?

At breakfast we joined our fellow guests and I shared my story with them. Then I asked Stephanie if any female guests had arrived at the inn after we went to bed. The answer was "no." And to think I didn't investigate!

After breakfast, Allanah and I joined Stephanie for one last chat. Stephanie mentioned that when Bill received the portrait of William Christie, only a few years before, it seemed as though his spirit came with the portrait. At the same time, the spirit of Mary Jane Christie took up using her nearby chair. Stephanie urged us to sit in the chair and look at the picture. The eyes seem to follow you around the room. You should stay there a night or two, and you will understand what others have said.

> Thank you for another wonderful stay. Jan and I find the Beild House to be the perfect "get away." We love it all … your hospitality, the uniqueness, the privacy, the security, the character, the food, the books, the charm, the service… and … of course, you extend the warmest welcome to us … we feel like friends. Thank you."

Our stay at Beild House was extraordinary. Although it was only one night, it rejuvenated me in ways you cannot imagine.

There's nothing like the personal touch. What can I say ... comfy, intimate, unique, caring, pampered, welcoming, the royal treatment all the way.

Those comments do wrap it all up.

The barefoot contessa, Stephanie if you prefer, will watch over your good health, your mind, and your spirit with the help of her great staff, her keen mind, and her bevy of spirits.

Strathmore House/Brookside Youth Centre

~ Cobourg ~

Who could she be, this woman in green velvet, strolling the grounds and hallways of Strathmore House? Where has she come from and why has she come? She has become known as the Green Lady of Strathmore. She is one of many spirits in this stately mansion on King Street E, in Cobourg, Ontario.

Strathmore House was built during the mid-1870s by George Mackenzie Clark. The house was designed in neoclassical style, with a formal three-bay symmetry on its primary south facade. It originally had a hipped roof with symmetrical brick chimneys, but that has been largely obscured by the remodelling and expansion of the house by a later owner.

Strathmore is one of only a few palatial summer homes that once lined Cobourg's streets.

George Clark was born in Belleville in 1828, and moved with his family to Cobourg as a young child. He was educated at Upper Canada College, and later studied law in the Cobourg office of Colonel D'Arcy Boulton.

A Ministry of Government Services report states,

After taking the bar, Clark proceeded to set-up a law partnership with W.H. Weller, son of W. Weller, three-time mayor of Cobourg and the owner of the Weller stagecoach line which ran between York [Toronto] and Kingston. In 1850, Clark married his partner's sister, Eliza Melissa Weller, and took up residence in Cobourg. They had four daughters, only two who lived into adulthood.

In 1857, Clark was appointed to the office of County Court Judge of Northumberland and Durham. The next year he was appointed junior judge. By 1882 he had become a senior judge. As a staunch Conservative supporter and personal friend of Sir John A. Macdonald, he was named chairman of a number of royal commissions; including the inquiry into all transactions connected with contracts and construction of the Canadian Pacific Railway. In 1887 he resigned his judicial offices and accepted the government's offer to become chief solicitor to the Canadian Pacific Railway.

His success in business was reflected in his home, Strathmore. In the 1871 Census of Cobourg, Clark was noted as owning a total of 1,050 acres of land. The Ministry of Government Services noted,

> Judge Clark had purchased the future site of Strathmore in 1869, as part of a 130 acre parcel of land in Concessions A & B, Lot 13, Hamilton Township. The greater portion of the land was immediately sold off in small parcels. The small 24 and one-half acre section in the south west corner of the south half of Lot 13, Concession A was retained and eventually mortgaged in 1874 for $3000. This was the future site of Strathmore.
>
> The exact date of the construction of Strathmore is unknown, however a house is indicated on the site in the 1878 Historical Atlas of Northumberland and Durham Counties.

The 1881 Census shows Judge Clark and his wife living in Hamilton Township that year. A Bell Telephone directory located the Clark residence on King Street E, probably at Strathmore.

Rob Mikel

An historic photograph depicting Strathmore at the time it was under private ownership.

Judge Clark retired in 1901, due to poor health. In June 1903 he placed a sale advertisement in the local newspaper, stating: "Strathmore, the residence of the subscriber, just east of town limits, 14 acres with a never-failing stream and pastures, gardens and gardener's dwelling, groves, barns, stables and other outbuildings. Main house, 14 rooms and all modern conveniences. George M. Clark."

The house failed to sell, and was rented out to Charles Donnelly of Pittsburgh, Pennsylvania, for the 1904 summer season. Donnelly purchased Strathmore that September for $12,500.

As a child, I spent many summers with my aunt and uncle, Chloris and Jack Heenan, and my cousins, Donna and Debbie, on Abbott Blvd. in Cobourg. I was aware of Strathmore and the other two mansions that stood at the top of the street. I recall stories about a ghost child who apparently had drowned in a pond on the grounds of Strathmore. People reported seeing her. Two of Judge Clark's daughters did not live to adulthood. Perhaps the young female spirit seen where a pond once was on the property is one of the daughters.

At the time Strathmore was built Cobourg was beginning to develop as an American resort town. The first American visitors were primarily naval and army officers and their families. Then the summer population began to include wealthy industrialists from Pittsburgh.

The Ministry of Government Services report adds:

> Initially interested in such business ventures as the railway from Cobourg to Peterborough and the Marmora iron mines, the Pittsburgh industrialists soon discovered Cobourg as a summer retreat and gradually began to build or renovate their own palatal summer residences particularly along King Street.
>
> Until the First World War, these Americans, mainly from Pittsburgh, formed the nucleus of one of the most fashionable American summer colonies (contemporaries sometimes compared Cobourg to Newport, Rhode Island).
>
> They came for six months of every year and brought servants, guests, and lavish lifestyles.

Charles Donnelly was a self-made Pittsburgh millionaire who had built his reputation in Western Pennsylvania railways. He also had extensive holdings in coal mines and real estate. He was a well-known art collector, and had eight children by the time he purchased Strathmore.

In 1905 he began substantial renovations that can still be seen today. The Brookside Youth Centre Building Studies describes the changes:

> The house more than doubled in size and became a much heavier, asymmetric American Colonial Revival house, which was popular at the time. The largest wing was added to the west of the original house, doubling the length of the hip roof and including a major two-storey columned portico and intermediate balcony. This portico focused on a new entry hall and grand staircase, and therefore, created an asymmetric, lake facade.

Charles Donnelly died in 1906, before the alterations were complete. His wife and eight children continued to summer in Cobourg. One daughter, Bessie, married into a prominent Cobourg family.

In 1913 the Donnelly family suffered several financial setbacks. Rumours persisted that they had used up an estate estimated at $14 million before bankruptcy was declared.

The Ministry of Government Services reported, "The Strathmore estate was in the Canadian courts until 1918, when it was finally sold to Stephen Haas of Toronto for $28,000." Mr. And Mrs. Haas continued to use Strathmore as a summer residence until the early 1940s.

In 1943 the entire estate was leased to the Ontario government to be used as a girl's training school. According to a ministry report,

> Cobourg seemed a logical location for the school since several large estates suited to the school's needs were readily available.
>
> The first house to be leased was the Willis McCook home on King Street E, in 1942 and then Strathmore in November, 1943. The Wallace H. Rowe estate, which stood between the McCook property and Strathmore, was acquired in 1951. The McCook estate and the Rowe estate were later demolished.

A description of the Strathmore property appeared in 1945:

> The property consists of 14.9 acres, about 10 of which are landscaped. There is a well-built house which now provides accommodation for 40 girls. There is also a combined coach house and gardener's house. The gardener's house section is now used as staff quarters. The coach house was converted to a gymnasium.
>
> In addition, in 1946 a plot plan of the estate indicates such other features as an icehouse; a playhouse; tennis courts; landscaping with a fountain; and a stream and two ponds located alongside the front drive.

In 1950 the government decided that these facilities were inadequate for girls. The girls were moved to another location, and the Cobourg facilities were made ready for a training school for junior boys. Today the

The grand staircase of Strathmore.

The landing on the staircase before reaching the second floor.

facility is known as Brookside Youth Centre, a secure-custody facility. The administration offices are located in Strathmore.

In the fall of 2014, I arrived at Strathmore to begin my research on the reported hauntings. Since Brookside Youth Centre and Strathmore are a secure-custody setting, I required government consent to be on site, tour the facility, and conduct interviews. Fortunately, Andrea Calvin, the deputy youth centre administrator of Brookside, was able to expedite that process. Thank you, Andrea!

I entered the lobby of Strathmore and picked up the wall phone that would connect me to central control, they notified the staff inside Strathmore, and I then gained entry. Kim Turner met me in the lobby. She was very friendly and extremely helpful. She had arranged for a number of staff working that day to meet with me in the boardroom, where I could conduct the interviews.

First, Kim took me on a tour of the building. Many of the rooms have been converted to offices. The front, southwest room still retains the elaborate plasterwork on the ceiling, but it is obscured by an inner office space. The present office for the administrator is the only room to remain intact from Strathmore's days as a private home. The grand staircase to the second floor was truly a piece of fine craftsmanship. The second floor is all offices.

The first person I interviewed was Chris McIvor, an employee at Brookside for the past twenty-nine years. He worked as a youth service officer in correctional services for eighteen years and then moved on to administrative duties.

Chris said, "My job, at first, was security. There was no fence around the building. We had youth living on the grounds. It was a secure-custody setting. The ongoing talk at work was about the spirit of a girl who had been murdered." He admitted that he never thought anything about it.

"At the time my job was to do security checks of the grounds and Strathmore. I had done all the checks here, but never had any unexplained experiences."

Not until 1990, during an interior security check. "One night I came into the building to do an interior check. As I was walking down the hall on the second floor I noticed two doors open. I closed and locked the doors. They should not have been open. I went back downstairs. As my foot landed on the last step I heard a 'bang, bang, bang.' The sound of doors slamming, hard enough to get my attention. It freaked me right out.

"There was nobody there! I phoned over to control to see if any of my fellow workers were playing a prank on me. I was told that all of the staff were at their work stations.

"This whole process happened in five minutes. I was nervous. All the outside doors were locked. I was alone in that building. I did another security check, and went to the second floor again. The two doors I had previously closed and locked were open again. All the other doors to the offices were closed and locked. Once more ... I closed and locked the two doors.

"I know there was a spirit there that night, in the building, but I have never had anything happen since then."

Next I interviewed Judy Tucker. Judy is the youth services manager. She has worked in the corrections field for thirty-six years, and been at Brookside for the past twenty-six years. I asked Judy if she had a story to tell about the spirits in Strathmore or in Brookside, which includes six buildings, or units, as they are called inside the fence. These units are where the youth reside, and each unit is named after a famous Canadian.

Judy shared a particular incident that occurred in her early years there. "I was working in the Carr unit on the grounds [the building is named after Emily Carr]. That night I received a call from my supervisor, telling me the light was on in the superintendent's house [shift supervisor's office]. This building is located in the middle of the fenced-in section of the property. I was playing cards with the staff and when I left I took the cards with me.

"When I entered the building, I went upstairs to turn the light off. I returned to the Carr Unit, but then realized that I had left my cards in the superintendent's house. Back I went, only to discover that the light was on and my deck of cards was completely spread out on the floor. No one else had been in that building. I picked up the cards and ran out of there, and left the darn light on!"

Judy had more encounters than that! "Sometimes I was on security patrol of Strathmore. The nursing station was, at that point in time, located in Strathmore. We were to sign the log book and check that the vault where the medication was stored was secure. We were also to check the rest of the building. As I opened the door to the medical centre a somber voice said, 'Welcome and good evening.' I was so startled. And then I realized that the radio had somehow turned itself on."

Then she discovered that the voice was connected to an ad, on the radio, for a funeral home! She knew the nurses would never have left the radio on. The time was 3:00 a.m., and she was spooked!

A year to two later she had another experience. "In the daytime staff training is often done in the board room in Strathmore. When I came on for evening security patrol, I noticed from the outside of Strathmore that that the lights were on in the boardroom." There were people in the boardroom — but they weren't any of the staff of Brookside Youth Centre!

"As I peered in the window of the boardroom, the lights went out. The boardroom had sensory lighting; the lights would only come on when someone entered the room.

"I entered the building and went to the boardroom. There was no one there. Then I checked the other office doors. No sign of anyone. No lights on. However, as I left the building, I noticed that the lights had come back on in the boardroom. I just kept on going."

Judy had many more stories, including a strange one that had happened a year ago to another co-worker by the name of Stephanie Wilson.

The boardroom in Strathmore, where the lights come on by themselves at night.

"Stephanie was working the night shift in the Bernier Unit, located in the far corner of the secure setting. That building contains nineteen rooms and is occupied by youth serving time."

Protocol dictates that security staff walk through the building twice an hour. One night, on her rounds, Stephanie was followed! "Stephanie was doing a security check and it was just after midnight. As she neared the end of the hallway she began to feel really uncomfortable and was sure there was someone or something behind her. She went to the manager and asked him to review the security camera footage."

This is what they saw: "As Stephanie gets to the end of the hallway, an orb of light comes out of the cement wall. It begins to look like a worm measuring about three inches in diameter. It drops to the floor behind her and then bounces back up in the air. It is right behind her, following her down the hall. As she nears the lounge it, vanishes into thin air.

"I always try to rationalize things. It is such an eerie feeling walking around here at night…. The Stephanie Wilson encounter was too much. I saw that film footage too. No flashlight could do that. It was definitely a big fat worm of light."

My next interview was with Jeannie Berrigan, a health-care manager. "Seven or eight years ago another nurse and I were standing by the printer in the medical centre in Strathmore. The two of us were having a discussion about something, when the printer came on and printed out a picture of a daisy with a line under the photograph that said, 'Anything is possible.'

"We tried to figure it out. No one had accessed the printer during our conversation!

"One other time that same co-worker was working alone at night in the medical centre. At nine p.m. she called over to the control office to enquire if there was anyone else in Strathmore. She was told she was the only one there in the building.

"She could hear furniture being moved around above her, on the second floor of the building. It sounded like someone dragging furniture."

Jeannie continued, "The medical centre is now in the fenced-in area of Brookside. We have only been there for five years. We often experience the smells of someone baking cookies in the building.

"One nurse smelled A535, which is an ointment used to treat sore muscles. We do not have this medication on site. This ointment would normally be used by an elderly person."

Technology seems to be affected by this spiritual activity. Jeannie adds, "Our computers act up a lot. Computer programs won't open up; we are often denied access; printers won't print; we call in a technician, and nothing is wrong. These are not old computers."

Other staff members have reported seeing full apparitions at Brookside. A gentleman in a top hat and tails is often seen in the Banting and Bernier units. He is also seen near the old carriage house and sometimes seen smoking a cigar. Nurses report odours of cigar smoke in the medical centre. The woman in green velvet who smells of lily of the valley is also a spirit of the place.

I asked Jeannie if she had ever heard the story about the drowning of a little girl in the pond. Although she had heard others tell the story, no one seems to have reported seeing the girl. Nevertheless, the story has persisted.

Valerie Robertson is an Ontario Provincial Police special constable who is stationed at Strathmore. She has seen a male spirit in the house. "This one day I went down into the basement ... I just wanted to have a look around. There was this mirror near the basement stairs. I glanced at [it] and saw what looked like a male figure. I also saw the number five in the mirror. What really surprised me was that the lettering font used for the number was exactly the same lettering type of my address number on my house."

Valerie's co-worker Constable Darren Edwards had an odd experience one day. Valerie described what happened: "Darren watched the coiled fire hose just outside our office begin to unravel before his eyes."

Valerie didn't stop there. "A man I worked with has had some experiences. He has watched a water tap turn on by itself and the main toilet flush on its own in the back bathroom. He has heard furniture being moved around, and he also claims to have seen the female spirit in the green dress by the side doors ... and windows that open up on their own."

She ended with this story: "One of the girls and I brought in a Ouija Board. We were in the kitchen on the second floor. The door there is always locked. As we began our Ouija session the lock on the kitchen door started to move and the sound tap, tap, tap. We asked the board, 'Is that you moving the lock?' The answer was yes!"

I was unable to answer my initial questions about the Green Lady of Strathmore, but I do know that something is happening there. The emotional energy of the troubled youth residing here may be triggering the technology; the lights, locks, and computers. There is a great deal of unexplained activity, a lot of history to the grounds, many stories experienced and shared, and no doubt a truth yet to be revealed.

Sharon Temple

~ Sharon ~

The Sharon Temple was designed to embrace the soul, to become one with universal spirit; to embrace peace. To this day, anyone stepping foot inside this temple can still feel the peace and joy established by the Children of Peace. It is also a place where many spirits have chosen to stay.

The temple is a museum site now, located in the village of Sharon, Ontario. In 1990 it was designated as a national historic site of Canada. The site itself is made up of eight distinctive heritage buildings that house upward of 6,000 artifacts. The property and buildings are made available for public use, tours, concerts, and weddings, through the Sharon Temple Museum Society.

To understand who the Children of Peace were, you have to know about their leader, David Willson. He was a theologist, a poet, a writer of hymns, and a political reformer. He was born on June 7, 1778, in Dutchess County, New York. He was the son of John and Catherine Willson, poor, pious Presbyterians.

David was fourteen years old when his father passed away, and David took on an apprenticeship with a carpenter. In 1801, David and his

Sharon Temple

The Sharon Temple as it appears today.

wife, Phoebe, and their two sons, John David and Israel, moved to Upper Canada. They walked north on a blazed trail, later to become Yonge Street, and settled on a new land grant, Lot 10, in the second concession of East Gwillimbury. This area of land later formed the core of the village of Hope, now the village of Sharon.

In 1805, David Willson joined the Quakers. His wife was already a member. But during the War of 1812, his preaching resulted in his banishment from this religious group. He formed the Children of Peace from the fellowship that supported his viewpoint.

According to Sharon Temple Museum Society,

> This group carried forward their core Quaker values of equality, charity, peace and education. These beliefs were foreign to the colonial authorities and the British Crown.
>
> Willson likened his group to the Old Testament Israelites, lost in the wilderness. They were fleeing a cruel and uncaring English pharaoh. They were to build the "new Jerusalem" prophesied in the book of Revelation. At the centre of their community, they determined to build a Temple, somewhat after the manner of Solomon.

Sharon Temple

These are the original seats, dating back to the time of the Children of Peace.

Sharon Temple

One of three organs built by Richard Coates on display at the temple.

Jacob's Ladder, the steep set of stairs that led to the musicians gallery on the second floor.

The temple was built square, unlike the Quaker meeting houses. The structure symbolized dealing "on the square" with all people; each side represented a cardinal post (east, south, west, north). A door was placed in the centre of each side, indicating equality to all who entered. Four pillars form a central square known as the Ark; the pillars symbolize the four precepts of the temple: faith, hope, love, and charity. In the centre of the Ark a bible sits, opened to the Ten Commandments. Twelve more pillars surround the Ark, one for each of the disciples of Jesus Christ. The temple is seventy feet high, in three diminishing storeys, symbolizing the Trinity.

Looking up you can see an ornate lantern, capped with four golden spires, located on each corner of every storey; these twelve lanterns, when illuminated, represent the twelve apostles going out into the world to bring salvation. At the centre top, suspended between four lanterns, there is a golden globe — this was the highest point in the village of Hope. Here they inscribed their highest vision: peace to the world.

David Willson was neither an architect nor master builder, however, he was the designer of the temple and of other meeting houses. He claimed his designs and their inspirations came from visions. The Sharon Temple Museum Society adds that,

[H]e did have a master builder named Ebenezer Doan. Ebenezer's creative techniques as an accomplished builder are beautifully demonstrated in the simple rock foundation, for the Temple, a foundation that does not even go below the frost line and yet the building remains structurally sound to this day. From Doan's first house [1819], the drive shed and the granary have been relocated to Temple grounds and fully restored.

David Willson had designed and prepared not only the form of the building but a timetable as well. Willson determined that since Genesis called for the construction of the world in six days with a seventh day to rest and observe the outcome, then this house [temple] should take six years to build with a seventh to rest and observe the outcome.

Author Emily McArthur, who wrote the text for a commemorative pamphlet in 1898, described the temple:

The first or ground floor, is the auditorium, sixty feet square. The second or middle storey is the music gallery where the band can render a selection of music while the congregation enters the building. The third storey is the dome, from which there is an open space to the ground floor.

On the evening of the first Friday of each September, the Temple is illuminated for divine worship, and presents a very beautiful appearance when lighted, there being 2,952 panes of glass in the windows and spires.

The building was intended to represent Christianity, enlightening the darkened understanding of the mind.

As for the contribution of the Children of Peace to society, Albert Schrauwers, author of an essay entitled "Union is Strength: From Moral Economy to Joint Stock Democracy" wrote,

More than a religious sect, the Children of Peace were economic and political innovators, helping to establish Canada's first farmers' cooperative and credit union.

Their system of mutual aid was based on labour exchanges [work bees], cooperative marketing, and a credit union. For those in immediate crisis, alms and a shelter for the homeless served as a stopgap. So successful was this cooperative regime of mutual aid that, by 1851, Hope was the most prosperous agricultural community in the province.

Music played an important role in the lives of the Children of Peace. Emily McArthur wrote,

> They differed from the Quakers in several peculiarities, they were fond of music and they introduced both vocal and instrumental music in their devotional exercises.
>
> In 1820 a brass band of music was organized in connection with the society and a pipe organ was introduced to the service.
>
> They began to cultivate their talent for singing in 1819, and engaged the best teachers available at the time.

The Sharon Temple Museum Societies' book *Rebuilding Hope, The Sharon Temple After 175 Years* highlighted the later years of the community:

> Age was taking its toll on the village patriarch, David Willson, now in his seventies. He could no doubt look back with pride at the accomplishments of a lifetime. But he would also have recognized that the religious community now generally known by his name, the Davidites, would pass with him. He remained the leader until his death in 1866.
>
> His son, John David, took up leadership of the Children of Peace. In 1876, the group re-incorporated as a

"charitable society" and in 1889, after the death or departure of Willson's sons, the Children of Peace faded away.
The Temple and its other meeting houses fell into disrepair.

Eventually, the second meeting house of the Children of Peace
was torn down for lumber. The Sharon Museum Society adds,

> In 1917, Dr. James L. Hughes became President of the
> York Pioneer and Historical Society. Hughes chal-
> lenged the York Pioneers: "As an historical Society we
> have important duties to perform. No other part of the
> great province of Ontario has contributed as largely to
> the development of Canada, as the district within the
> boundaries of our Association has. Our forefathers
> were men of strong character, high purpose, and clear
> vision. By their devotion, and by their wisdom they laid
> the foundations of the educational, the financial, the
> municipal and the religious institutions of our country."
> In the midst of war, Dr. Hughes found the support to
> transform the Temple into one of the first acts of historic
> preservation in Canada. Hughes raised $1,500 to pur-
> chase the Temple, which was reopened on September 7,
> 1918, the traditional fall feast day of the Children of Peace.

On the grounds of the temple you can tour David Willson's study,
which was completed in 1829. This is where Willson wrote his hymns,
sermons, books, and pamphlets. Near this building is a white frame
cookhouse, originally located next to the second meeting house. Here
the Children of Peace prepared their feasts. Next is the Exhibit Building,
which outlines the significant role the Children of Peace had to play in the
struggle for democracy and social justice in early Canada. Beyond this
building is a log house, once the home of bandmaster Jesse Doan and
his family. Across the lawn is the Ebenezer Doan house. Built in 1819,
it is furnished as it might have appeared in the 1850s. Ebenezer and his
wife, Elizabeth, lived in the house with their son David and granddaugh-
ter Esther Ann. Behind the house you can see David Willson's cylindrical
outhouse.

Sharon Temple

David Willson's study, where he meditated and wrote his music and books.

Visitors to the Sharon Temple often comment on the peace they feel here. They feel they are not alone; they are in the company of the Children of Peace. When you sit still in the temple you may hear their music playing in the background — many visitors do!

Megan Houston, program and site co-ordinator, knows about the stillness of the temple. She describes it: "It is just silent. I have never felt a silence like that before. There is no hum of electricity. It is also a heavy silence. There is nothing around. You don't even hear crickets at night. It is as if the building is intentionally blocking out all the noise from the outside."

Megan admits that every once and a while the silence is broken. "Two or three tourists a year tell me that they heard music being played when touring the temple."

Some of these tourists are direct descendants of the Children of Peace. The second weekend of August is Heritage Weekend. Megan says that more than one hundred descendants arrive for this occasion. These family connections may very well stir up some spiritual connection with the past.

Megan, standing in the doorway of David Willson's study.

Megan admits that there is paranormal activity in all the buildings. She says, "The temple is full of happiness, peace and light. You might be having a terrible day, but when you enter the temple it's as if someone has hugged you. All your cares just dissipate. You just feel the spirits there.

"You can especially sense the spirits after catering a wedding, all the people have left, and you're here alone, at 3:00 a.m."

In August 2010, the singer Loreena McKennitt arrived at the temple to record her album, *The Wind that Shakes the Barley*. Megan described what that was like: "Loreena and the recording crew were here for seven days. It was quite magical. The acoustics in the temple are incredible."

Loreena talked about how inspiring the setting was to her. She said, "There is a fascinating interplay between architecture and sound, visually and sonically. The temple inspired us all."

During the Fall Lantern Light tour in October of 2010, a sorority group toured the Sharon Temple. Sonia Law and her daughter were part of the group, and had an unexplained experience while touring the Doan House. They had just finished visiting the upstairs of the house, and had returned to the downstairs kitchen. Suddenly they heard a big bang in the upstairs bedroom. They had been the last people to leave the upstairs.

Sometimes it is not the spirits and the buildings, but the artifacts that create an atmosphere. According to Megan: "For example, in the log house [Jesse Doan's home], people sense some spirit activity around the loom that is set up in the cabin. In the cookhouse, visitors report hearing people preparing food and ladies laughing."

Megan recalled being on a tour with some ladies from the Hedge Witch store, located just down the road from the temple. "When the group arrived at David Willson's Study, one lady said they were not going in there. They were feeling very unwelcome."

The Ebenezer Doan House appears to be occupied by someone from the past. Megan explains, "In 2010, one visitor said they saw a lady in the upstairs window. She was a young lady, wearing an old-fashioned plain, dark dress."

Megan will admit that she is not a very intuitive person, but when it comes to the Ebenezer Doan House, she feels uncomfortable. She described what happened to one employee in this house. "It was later in the day and one of our workers was vacuuming the Doan House. She was suddenly overtaken with a feeling that somebody was starring at her. It made her feel uncomfortable.

The Ebenezer Doan House, built in 1819.

"Ten minutes later she returned to the office. The vacuum cleaner remained in the middle of the room. This confirmed my own earlier feelings."

I went down the street to visit the Hedge Witch and meet owner Diane King. Diane was quite welcoming, and directed me to her office. She has been in business here for fourteen years. The store is like a spiritual Baskin Robbins, offering a host of flavours, from candles to jewellery to books. Diane also has several gifted psychics who do readings for customers on a daily basis. I would describe her as a seeker of the truth.

This building was a general store when the Children of Peace lived in Hope (Sharon). Diane adds, "There once was a graveyard situated behind the store. A couple of tombstones were still visible in the early 1900s." There is no evidence of a graveyard today, but the original meeting house of the Children of Peace was once just south of the store.

Diane has been on the Spirit Walk at the Sharon Temple. While in the temple she heard something. "I was in the northwest corner of the building when I heard a woman's choir singing." She later discovered that this was the area of the temple where the women's choir sang.

Diane talked about feeling the presence of spirits on the far west side of the property. She sensed there was once a cemetery there. There is,

Diane King, on the left, owner of the Hedge Witch, with her daughter, Megan Rooney.

however, no record of a graveyard having been in that location. She also mentioned sensing the presence of soldiers.

When I first met Diane she mentioned feeling the presence of a spirit in her building, where she has both her store and living quarters. One spirit is a tall male, wearing a black frock coat. She feels his presence in the upstairs hallway.

Her sister, Donna King, has what I call the gift of sight. Donna is able to see spirits and sense the spirit energy or the energy imprinting of buildings and the land. I was interested to hear what Donna had to say about the Sharon Temple and the grounds, including her sister's store. At one time Donna also lived above the store. "One day I walked into my sister's store and was overcome by a musty, leather smell. Diane had picked up on the smell, as well. The smell is associated with the spirit of a man who was called the captain. He grew up in a mansion across the street from the store. I believe he was there because this is where he would have picked up his mail when the building was a general store.

"He wasn't actually a captain, but that's what people called him. He went to fight in the Civil War and lost his life on one of the Great Lakes. I believe he only shows up in association with the anniversary of his death or his birthday."

Donna has actually seen the full apparition of the man that her sister senses, in the upstairs hallway of the building. "He is a tall man wearing a black frock coat. He has long hair, pulled back into a ponytail. He has no facial hair. He does not know why he is there in this time frame. Every time he appears he paces back and forth. It is like he is waiting for something to happen. He is either waiting for a child to be born or someone is ill in the house.

"I have also seen a young girl, aged eight or ten, wearing a nightgown and a lace cap tied under her chin. She has blonde hair."

I thought it was rather a busy place for Donna to live — not very restful!

"I often hear a bell ringing downstairs. In the days when the building was a general store, the owners would have had a bell on the door. Every time someone entered the building, the bell would have been rung. I also hear voices downstairs."

Donna also spoke to me about the Sharon Temple. "I do not necessarily pick up on spirits, but rather the energy associated with the buildings or the grounds. I have seen a blacksmith shop located in the front left section of the property by the parking lot. I saw a blacksmith kneel down, shoeing a large draft horse, and get kicked in the head. He died from the injury."

Donna commented on the loom that Megan had spoken of. "There is a lot of energy around the loom. It is somehow connected with someone who worked the loom. The person did not want to be weaving. I sense something similar to slave labour."

One area of the property, already mentioned to me by Diane, was an overgrown area on the extreme west side of the property, behind the temple. "I sense the presence of soldiers and Natives buried here. I did connect with three Confederate soldiers in the area. I was unable to communicate with them. They were quite agitated. They are buried here."

Donna could be right about the Confederate soldiers. Thousands of residents of what is now Canada left to fight in the Civil War. Confederate generals were known to have meetings in Ontario during the war.

Donna gave me one more story, about a ringing bell. She told me I needed to talk to Diane again. Diane told me, "A few years ago I received a shipment of Tibetan bells. We decided to ring one bell to see what the tone was like. Angela, a psychic/medium, was here in the store at the time. As I was ringing the bell, Angela could see a group of men with beards and wearing black hats walk into the store."

The ringing of the bell had brought the Children of Peace back from the past!

"They always rang a bell to have everyone gather at the meeting house. Remember the meeting house was just south of this building. I have never rung a bell in the store again."

When asked about the Sharon Temple, Angela spoke of a disturbing male presence in the Doan House. She believes there are bodies buried on the property.

The Sharon Temple, the Hedge Witch store, and the community of Sharon are still connected to the Children of Peace and to David Willson. Their historical and spiritual presence is still visible and audible to community members and visitors. It is truly a place to embrace and connect, not just with the universal spirit!

Readers' Response

One of the most wonderful aspects of being a writer is reader response. When it comes to writing ghost stories, the reader response is not only incredible, but worth printing. Many people have stories of their own to share.

Thank you to everyone who has written to me. Your leads and marvellous words, and your generosity to take the time to write your stories, is appreciated. In honour of your efforts, here are a few I'd like to share with you.

HAUNTED CHURCH
Stratford

Dear Mr. Boyle:

I first read your two books of Ontario ghost stories last October when we were visiting relatives in Bracebridge. I thought at the time of writing to you, but didn't. On rereading your books this week, I decided to write. I found them both fascinating.

I have always been interested in the supernatural, and have collected "ghost" stories all my life, but I never had a personal experience with the supernatural until 1994.

My wife of twenty-seven years died suddenly in March that year and I was deeply depressed. Later that spring a colleague at the Canadian Museum of Civilization, where I had worked, suggested that we visit Stratford. He stayed at a B&B (which turned out to be run by one of my wife's elementary-school teachers) and I stayed with a friend who was the minister at the old Presbyterian church near the land registry office.

There are two Presbyterian churches in downtown Stratford; this is the older of the two. It is a huge, labyrinthine building, which has had several additions over the years, hence has many levels and corridors.

My friend explained to me that the church had been built on the site of a cemetery. All the graves that were known were moved, but there were a number of unmarked graves, including those of some murderers hung at the county gaol, which occupied part of the site. When excavation began, human remains were unearthed.

The church is reputed to be haunted and he told me that, several times over the years, he had heard people walking and in some cases running on the floor over his office, when he was working there at night. On one occasion, he heard footsteps come down the hall toward the office. He looked at the door and saw the door knob turn. He jumped up and opened the door, but there was nothing there.

I found all this interesting and very credible, as my friend is a pretty hard-headed individual, not given to fantasy.

One of the church officers was there when we arrived. We conversed for a few moments, then he left. My friend made sure the door was locked behind him, then proceeded to take me on a tour of the church. We were about three levels up, in the towers, where he was showing me their sound system, when the fire alarm went off. We hastened back to his office, where he called the fire department to report that we were in the church but could see no evidence of fire.

While he was on the telephone, I was standing outside his door and noticed that the fire alarm on the wall next to his door had been pulled and that the little glass bar was lying on the floor, in two pieces. I called this to his attention while we waited for the fire department. As the door near his office was still locked, we had to admit the firemen, who were accompanied by a police officer.

With them, we checked every room in the church, tried every door, they were all locked, and every window, likewise. There was no explanation for the fire alarm. After the firemen had left, we made a second inspection with the police officer. We were all perplexed. When she asked what she was supposed to put in her report, my friend said, "Well, I strongly suggest you don't attribute it to the ghosts!"

The Scent of Perfume

As I said, my dear wife's death depressed me profoundly, but I must say that I have never once questioned the reason for her death. I have always felt that God had a purpose in it. That has not made me less sad and lonely. Some weeks following her death, I was feeling very low. I went into our bedroom, sat down on her side of the bed and wept. Suddenly the air was filled with the scent of her perfume. It was very striking. I sat there amazed for perhaps a minute, then left the room and immediately re-entered it. The scent was gone.

My daughter and my wife's sisters had cleaned out all my wife's clothes and other belongings, including her perfume, weeks before. No drawers had been opened and I had done absolutely nothing that could account for the scent of her perfume.

I may say that I felt very close to my wife at that moment, if astounded, and was very comforted. It was as if she had come to reassure and comfort me. In the next two years, I had four or five similar experiences, always in the same place except on one occasion when I was walking to the bus stop, on a route she had taken many times walking to a nearby mall, and I smelled her perfume outdoors. The closest person was perhaps 100 yards away and was downwind from me. Each time, the scent seemed weaker than the previous.

Some months went by and I assumed I would not smell the scent again. In April 1997, I had been on a trip to France and Belgium and I returned home. My children had moved out by now, both our dogs were dead, and I came home to a very quiet house. I went into the bedroom and said out loud, "Well, Brenda, I'm home!" Suddenly, but faintly, I smelled the perfume.

I have only smelled it once since then. In May 1998 a lady whom I met moved in with me. In June 1999, my daughter, who had a very special, close relationship with my wife, was married. It was a wonderful wedding and the reception, at the National Arts Centre, was spectacular. My companion and I returned home following the reception. Sue was somewhere else in the house. I was in the bedroom, sitting on my side of the bed and I was thinking, "Oh, Brenda, if only you could have been there!" And there was the perfume again, light and fleeting, only for a few seconds. I have not smelled it since.

L. Needham

THE DONNELLY HOMESTEAD
Lucan

Dear Mr. Boyle:

My wife and I have long enjoyed your "Discover Ontario" radio program and yesterday we bought your book *Haunted Ontario*. To be perfectly frank I'm a bit of a skeptic when it comes to the paranormal but the index entry of six pages on the Donnellys caught my attention. I have had a thirty-year-old fascination with the Donnelly story during which time I had many talks with Ray Fazakas, the author of *The Donnelly Album*, and corresponded for a while with Nora Lord, who was William Donnelly's daughter and who died in Sudbury on 22 September, 1975, at age 88.

In June 1997 we paid a visit to Rob and Linda Salts' place on the Roman Line. We did the tour of the property, something I had wanted to do for years but the previous owner was hostile to the idea of visits from strangers and kept the property posted.

Rob, who claims to be a psychic, certainly has no doubts about the presence of spirits in his home and barn. And something happened while we were there to shake my scepticism, at least somewhat.

On page 86 of your book you relate that people touring the site often mention that something touched them on the shoulder while no one was standing near them. I had a similar experience. While Rob was leading us from the house to the murder scene, I felt something brush across the top of my hair. I patted the top of my head very gingerly so as to dislodge it without getting stung, but there was nothing there. Then the same thing happened again. This time I ran the fingers of both hands through my hair but came up with nothing. I didn't mention this to anyone at the time but a week or two later I wrote to Rob telling him about it.

Bill Burns

THE HAUNTING OF QUEEN'S UNIVERSITY RADIO STATION
Kingston

Dear Mr. Boyle:

I received your *Haunted Ontario* for Christmas and my holidays are now spoken for. It's well written, and fun. My wife bought it for me, as she knows I love Ontario history.

Can someone haunt a radio transmitter? This doesn't involve spectres or ghostly figures, but it does strongly suggest communication from beyond. Your story of Mr. E.B. Sutton, Bala Bay Hotel, prompted the memory, with his knockings on the hotel front door.

Before I go on, I should say that I really don't believe in spirits, ghosts, or things that go bump in the night. In fact, I hold no super, and think most of this haunted stuff is bunk. Granted, some interesting things have happened, so I maintain an open mind. I certainly don't have an explanation for what happened in your book. Nor what happened to me at CFRC.

Queen's University established the second radio station in Canada in 1923. They have published a book describing its history, however, the key thing to know is that it all started as an experiment in the electrical engineering department. Radio broadcasting was in its infancy then, and Queen's EE was on the forefront when they built a transmitter and went on the air. They broadcast from Fleming Hall, from a room on the upper floor. Two professors and a graduate student started the station. Professor D.M. Jemmett was the key person, who had the idea and got things going.

By the time I graduated in 1974 from Electrical, CFRC was fifty years old, and Professor Jemmett had retired, and was in poor health.

The station still operated its transmitter on the second floor of Fleming Hall with the antennas on the roof. This has all since been replaced.

I was the station engineer, although it was largely a voluntary job involving starting the transmitters, and checking them regularly. I took it quite seriously, though, as I was a keen ham operator, and had worked as engineer at CHFI, CFTR and CBC. I liked working with the old 1946 RCA transmitter, and knew its gut intimately.

The fall of 1973 saw me in graduate studies in electrical, and volunteering as station engineer and doing some announcing. Late on Thursday night, I returned to my downtown apartment late to get a cup of tea, and wind down from an evening studying on campus. It was your classic dark and stormy night, with a cold wind and rain. When I got a call from Mary Lou Keating at the station I was not too keen on getting on my bicycle, and heading back to campus. However, she said that the AM signal was off the air, the original CFRC was AM of course, while FM soldiered on.

It was about 12:15 a.m., but I was keen enough to go back and let myself in to a dark Fleming Hall. This place was built in the 1800s and was spooky even in the daytime. On the third floor the transmitter room was dark, and sure enough, the AM set was off the air. The power was on, and all the tubes were glowing, but it was deader than dead. I opened it up, and could find no fault. The set had tripped off by itself, and just wouldn't start. After about an hour, I still couldn't reset it, so headed home. Working on high voltage alone at night is never a good idea, and this big old RCA was not cooperating.

The next morning, I arrived before my first class, only to find that all classes were cancelled that morning. No explanation. I used the time profitably to find the fault in the AM transmitter. It took three hours and it was a real sleuth job. Despite being an experienced transmitter engineer, this fault was the hardest, and weirdest that I had seen. An insulated wire, buried deep in the guts, had been pushed up against a high voltage terminal. The insulation had been burned off, and the two were welded together. This could only happen if you had the power on, and were rubbing one against the other. No person could do this, as the power would go off once you opened the doors. For the life of me, I couldn't figure out why it would happen, let alone after thirty years of loyal service.

I closed everything back up and made things ready to go back on the air. Finally emerging from the transmitter room, I learned the reason for the class cancellations. The night before, about 11:30 p.m., Professor

Jemmett had died at Kingston General Hospital. KGH is across the quadrangle from Fleming Hall.

Being curious, I ran the logger tape back. This tape recorder takes its audio feed from a radio receiver, and would show the time of disruption. At 11:56 p.m. Mary Lou gave a time check. Four minutes later, the tape went dead.

A bizarre fault, at midnight, on the eve that Professor Jemmett died. I don't know. Sounds spooky to me. It's not just the timing that gets me; it's that no human hands could have created that fault, unless they were already inside the transmitter cabinet, which is not possible.

Ian Baines

P.S. One evening I was returning to my room in Northern France, and crossed an old First World War battlefield. I had been to many such places, and they hold no fear for me. However, as darkness fell, I was aware of hundreds of other people around me. My skin went cold, and I had to fight the urge to run. There was nobody there, just a dark woods with old trenches and wire. But, I'll tell you, I was not alone on that field. There was no doubt in my mind of that. That kind of makes me wonder.

TWO HAUNTED HOUSES
Port Hope & Whitby

Dear Mr. Boyle:

I have two stories to relate to you: a haunted house in Port Hope, and a haunted school in Whitby.

The Haunted House in Port Hope

A house on Dorset Street, in Port Hope, is quite haunted. At one point a man is said to have murdered his family in the home. I have heard this took place around 1870, but I would hesitate to put money on the year.

I have been told that the house was constructed back in the 1800s sometime. It was possibly the servant's quarters for one of the large estates that line the upper south side of Dorset Street. The house on the south side that housed servants across the road has been turned into a day spa. The original idea was to turn it into a bed and breakfast as I understand.

However, the idea of a spa came into being during renovations. Supposedly the work crew couldn't stand the noises and screaming they heard.

My brother-in-law, Stacy, used to cut grass on an adjoining property. He says that he always found he made himself go faster when cutting the portion of the lawn between the two houses. He says things just don't feel right there. He didn't know about the supposed haunting at the time.

Later Stacy met a person, through the drummer in his band, that is believed to have seen the ghosts haunting the house on Dorset. He will say very little about what he saw except to say that what is in there is very real. Stacy recounted in front of this person that he heard the ghost appears at the bottom of the basement stairway holding the heads of two young children. The ghost is also rumoured to travel toward the person seeing the apparition.

The Haunted School in Whitby

A friend of mine works at a school in Whitby. She is a believer in spirits and the supernatural. She believes there are at least two ghosts, maybe three, residing in the school. Her husband also believes this. He says he gets a strange feeling sometimes when he picks her up from the school.

Some of the children have seen the ghosts, according to my friend. One day two little girls sent a chill into their teacher. Most of the children were out at recess when one of the girls asked the teacher, "Who is that lady standing next to you?"

The teacher looked over and saw no one there. She asked what the girl was talking about.

The girl spoke up, "Yes, there she is and she's wearing a really pretty dress."

Children are sometimes excited because ghosts are helping them at the chalk board or playing with them by moving the chalk around. These ghosts seem friendly and even playful.

There is supposed to be another presence in the basement. Not a nice one. My friend asked her husband to accompany her down to the storage room area in the basement to get some supplies for her classroom the next day. She will not go into the basement alone if at all possible. He says he understands why; the feeling is creepy. She will buy supplies that she could otherwise get for free so long as it allows her to avoid the basement.

Dan Araujo

HAUNTED COTTAGE IN BOWMANVILLE

Dear Mr. Boyle:

I have a story to tell, which I have never been able to forget. My husband and I bought a cottage back in 1996. It was on Lake Ontario in the town of Bowmanville, Ontario. The house was in bad need of repair and we did a lot of work on it. We started by replacing the windows.

It was a bright sunny day when I arrived home after work. My husband met me at the door and noticed that my blood sugars were low. I am diabetic. I was given a glass of juice and was sitting on the couch in front of the large window that looks over the lake.

I was sharing my day with my husband when I caught what I thought at the time was the reflection of a man walking past the window. He was wearing a plaid shirt and coveralls. Just what an old-fashioned farmer would wear. I stopped in mid-sentence and was surprised when my husband said he did not see the man. I went out onto the deck where the man had to have walked in order for him to pass the window.

You see, I really saw him in the mirrors that were on the wall I was facing. This meant that he was actually in the house when I saw him. I was shaken from the experience and started to cry. I blamed it on my low blood sugar and dismissed it. I saw my neighbour a short time later and was telling him of my experience and he said that this had been farm land at one time.

The last time this happened to me was the year my step-daughter got married. We had also sold the house and were packing up and getting ready for the wedding. We had a garden party the day after the wedding and it was bright and sunny. We were in and out of the house and the guests were outside under tents set up on the property.

The party was winding down and there were only a few guests left when I felt I needed some juice. I went into the house. I was coming out of the bathroom when I looked across the hall into the spare room that was full of boxes. There, bending over one of the boxes, was a lady in a long black dress. She looked up at me as I came through the door, but she seemed to look through me, as though I was not there. I stood there, just staring at her. I came out to where my guests were and they knew something had happened. I told them what I had seen and I started to cry. They were certain that I was upset and very frightened, but I think they had a hard time believing me.

I know what I saw and what I have experienced since living in that house and I can't explain it. It was as though they wanted me to know they were there and maybe because we were changing things, this caused them to show themselves. I don't know.

For some strange reason I was able to feel and see things only when my blood sugars were low and only when I lived in that house. It has been two years now since we moved and I have had low blood sugar episodes since, but no ghostly encounters.

Readers name withheld by request.

HAUNTED HOUSE
Etobicoke

Dear Mr. Boyle:
A friend has just recently introduced me to one of your books. I was quickly captivated and read it in a day. Then I read it again.

My friend, Laura, who actually gave me two of your books, has known me for about twenty-five years. We've been early childhood friends. We grew up one block from each other. Laura knows about the house I grew up in. She never liked it much. We'd usually play at her house.

You see, not a day went by without an incident in my house. It was typical to see plants moving and the television would go off and on. The lights did the same thing. We heard footsteps, loud and clear. There were doors that shut, or muffled voices, and most often our stuff would simply disappear! Small things, but not very often would they reappear. I always said that one day we would find all our missing belongings stashed away somewhere in that house. Of course, we never did.

My brothers, being older, were scared, but tried not to show it. I kept a diary for two solid years, until one day even it went missing.

We never really felt alone in that house. We children would discuss it among ourselves. Dad wouldn't hear of it. Mom would just say we were imagining things.

The basement was the worst. Our cats would not go down there. If we made them they would freeze with their backs hunched up and their hair on end.

Once we accidentally shut the basement door with one cat downstairs. It went missing all day. At night we were in the basement because we could hear her meowing. We eventually found her between the ceiling and the floor, above our heads. We could not figure that one out.

My birthday is in June and when I was little my Mom would have a pool party for me. All my friends were there. One year, one of my friends went downstairs through the side door to use the washroom. She came up right away, crying and screaming. She wanted my mom to call her mom to come and take her home.

Even though all kinds of strange things happened there we never knew the extent of it until my parents finally sold the house.

On that day my mother arrived and took my husband and me out to dinner. She started off by saying, "You know how you kids always thought the house was haunted? So I lied! It really was haunted and the first time I saw the ghost I almost died. I thought we were being robbed."

She finally told us what she had seen. It was very late at night and mom and dad were in bed. Dad was asleep and mom was reading. Suddenly a man came into the bedroom. My mom froze. She knew dad was snoring and couldn't do a thing. She thought they were being robbed. So she pretended she was sleeping, too, and hoped he wouldn't hurt anyone. He seemed so real. My mom blinked a little and slowly opened her eyes. He faded away.

My mom told me about all the different times she would see him. He would be sitting on the porch when she got home from work. She would see him in the hallway or downstairs in the laundry room.

My old house is haunted. I truly believe it now. The strange part, though, is our neighbours had strange occurrences in their houses, too. My childhood friend, Cindy, who lived next door, said her mom felt the same way about their home. I only found this out last week.

Cindy told me that, as a child, she heard the voices of English-accented women having a tea party. This was heard only on weekends. Crosses would appear in the windows.

We also remembered another house on the street that was rumoured to be haunted. Could our whole street have been haunted?

Dana Gallant

GHOSTS OF WORLD WAR I

Dear Mr. Boyle:

You say in your books that when you enter certain areas you can almost feel a presence. For me, in many ways, this is an everyday occurrence. Not the seeing of things, but the feeling of things.

Everyone in my family is either able to see or feel the unknown. Then there are the family members who can do both. There have been experiences reported by family members for over a hundred years. My grandfather had them. When he was little, during the First World War, he woke up to find a headless soldier at the foot of his bed. The headless soldier turned out to be his uncle, who was away at war. His uncle appeared to him at the exact moment of his death.

My other grandfather had an experience when my mom was about five years old. He came running out of his bedroom crying, "Annie help me, they're coming through the walls after me."

My grandfather had been a sniper in the First World War. What I believe he saw were the men he had killed. My grandmother simply walked into their room and said a prayer of absolution, banishing all that was not of God from their room. After that my grandfather was able to sleep without the nightmares that had plagued him since the war.

May Cuing

DEAD SON RETURNS
Ottawa

Dear Mr. Boyle:

I found your book *Haunted Ontario* in my local library. I made the mistake of reading it when my kids were asleep and my husband was out. I enjoyed the depth of your research and the way it was presented. It did, however, scare the bejeepers out of me.

Since I enjoyed your book so much I decided to write you with my own story.

My own story requires a bit of background, so please bear with me. I grew up in a neighbourhood in south Ottawa. At the age of ten I acquired a paper route. I delivered the *Ottawa Citizen* newspaper for about four years. I was also playing hockey at the time and most of my "paper" money went to the costs of hockey. Every two weeks I was required to collect money owing to the *Citizen* from my customers. Hockey also gave out raffle tickets to each player to try to sell, also to make the cost less for parents.

I naturally asked my customers to support my hockey and they gave generously over the years. One year it seemed that I had a lot of raffle tickets to sell and since I was getting tired of asking my customers I decided to try a different street.

I was about thirteen years old and it was on a Wednesday night that I rang the doorbell of a particular house. "Good evening, my name is Heidi Metcalfe and I was wondering if you would like to support my hockey team by buying a raffle ticket?"

The gentleman looked about thirty, clean shaven, friendly and about 5'8", light hair, a sweater and a pair of blue jeans. He told me that his parents were out of town but would be back the next Wednesday. He said that they always supported minor hockey teams and would certainly buy a ticket. I thanked him and went on my way.

Having some experience in selling raffle tickets I went back the following Wednesday. A gentleman, about fifty or sixty, answered the door. He looked almost like the gentleman of a week before only older. I told him that I was there last week and what must have been his son told me to come back this night.

He didn't say anything at first and then said that I must be mistaken. I described the man of a week before and told him that he said his parents were out of town but to come in a week. He turned really pale and said that he was at his son's funeral the week before.

I was shocked and I apologized. I went straight home after that and did not bother that family anymore.

Sincerely,

Heidi Metcalfe

THE DONNELLY WOMEN

Not sure how to start this letter, so I'll jump right in ... I was at the Cobourg Waterfront Festival and bought your book *Haunted Ontario*. I was drawn to your booth. I am glad, because the book I bought had a section about my relatives in it. It was wonderful hearing another version of what happened ["The Black Donnellys of Lucan"]. Everything I have found so far was the same old boring story — the Donnellys were evil, terrorized the neighbourhood, blah, blah, blah.

As a point of interest I wanted to share a few things about this family that have never been in print.

1. The relatives of the Donnellys (female anyway) frequently get visits from them. Each time it's benevolent; like the rest of us, yes they can have a temper, but it only shows when threatened.
2. You mentioned some "experiences" by tourists that wasn't surprising — we all love music and have an urge to touch everything, it's an affection thing that we all have.
3. All the women in this family have psychic abilities; the most recent case is my niece. When she was four (average age of onset) she would visit with my great-grandmother (who died years before she was born). My niece would repeat phrases and describe how she looked down to a T. And, no there were no pictures of my great-grandmother for her to reference. No one ever talks about these things for fear of being called nuts. But, privately, we all develop our skills so that, like our ancestors, we can look over future generations.
4. The name James and Joanne [Johannah] are still passed down.

I hope this adds to your experience of the [Black] Donnellys. It has been a tradition that is far from over — be it in a good way.

If You Would Like to Visit

Blinkbonnie Harbour Inn
50 Main Street
Gananoque, Ontario
613-382-7272/800-265-7474

Grafton Village Inn
10830 Country Road 2
Grafton, Ontario
905-349-3024
www.graftonvillageinn.ca

MacKechnie House Bed & Breakfast
173 Tremaine Street
Cobourg, Ontario
905-372-6242
www.mackechniehouse.com

The University of Toronto
St. George Campus, 27 King's College
Circle
Toronto, Ontario
www.utoronto.ca

The Hockey Hall of Fame
30 Yonge Street
Toronto, Ontario
416-360-7765
www.hhof.com

Joseph Brant Museum
1240 North Shore Blvd E.
Burlington, Ontario
905-634-3556
www.museumsofburlington.com/
joseph-brant

Emma's Back Porch
2084 Old Lakeside Road
Burlington, Ontario
905-634-2084
www.emmasbackporch.ca

Fort George
Superintendent, Niagara National
Historic Sites
Box 787
Niagara-on-the-Lake, Ontario
905-465-4257
www.pc.gc.ca/fortgeorge

Kyle Upton — Ghost Tours of Fort George
ghosttours@hotmail.com

Legg's Historic General Store (Birr)
23204 Richmond Street, North
R.R. 42
London, Ontario
519-666-0759

The Albion Hotel
1 Main Street
Bayfield, Ontario
519-565-2641
www.thealbionhotel.ca

Avon Theatre
99 Downie Street
Stratford, Ontario
519-271-1600
www.stratfordfestival.ca

Mylar & Loreta's Restaurant
Highway 24
Singhampton, Ontario
705-445-1247
www.mylarandloretas.ca

Gravenhurst Opera House
295 Muskoka Road, South
Gravenhurst, Ontario
705-687-5550
888-495-8888
www.gravenhurst.ca/en/opera/opera.asp

Ghost Tours of Gravenhurst Opera House with Terry Boyle
entwood@vianet.ca

Calhoun Lodge
Massasauga Provincial Park
380 Oastler Park Drive
Parry Sound, Ontario
705-378-2401
www.ontarioparks.com/park/themassasauga

Ojibway Club
PO Box 250
Pointe-au-Baril, Ontario
705-366-5085
www.ojibwayclub.com

Old Barber House Restaurant
5155 Mississauga Rd.
Mississauga, Ontario
905-858-7570
www.oldbarberhouse.com

Oakville Museum at Erchless Estate
8 Navy Street
Oakville, Ontario
1-905-338-4400
www.oakvillemuseum.ca

Beild House Country Inn and Spa
64 Third Street
Collingwood, Ontario
1-705-444-1522, 1-888-322-3453
www.beildhouse.com

The Sharon Temple Museum Society
Sharon Temple
18974 Leslie Street
Sharon, Ontario
905-478-2389
www.sharontemple.ca

Bibliography

Brambilla, Giovan Battista, Gianni Mercurio, Stefano Petricca, eds. *Marilyn Monroe: The Life, the Myth*. New York: Rizzoli, 1995.

Chandler, Charlotte. *Nobody's Perfect: Billy Wilder, a Personal Biography*. Toronto: Simon & Shuster, 2002.

Colombo, John Robert. *Haunted Toronto*. Toronto: Dundurn, 1996.

Crow, Cameron and Billy Wilder. *Conversations with Wilder*. New York: Alfred A. Knopf, 1999.

Davies, Blodwen. *Paddle and Palette: The Story of Tom Thomson*. Toronto: Ryerson Press, 1930.

Fazakas, Ray. *The Donnelly Album*. Toronto: Firefly Books, 1995.

Guiles, Fred Lawrence. *Legend: The Life and Death of Marilyn Monroe*. London, U.K.: Scarborough House Publishers, 1991.

Harvey, James. *Movie Love in the 50s*. New York: Alfred A. Knopf, 2001.

Hawke, William. *Historic Gananoque*. Belleville, ON: Mika Publishing, 1974.

Kael, Pauline. *For Keeps: 30 Years at the Movies*. New York: Dutton, 1994.

Leadbeater, C.W. *The Other Side of Death: Scientifically Examined and Carefully Described*. Whitefish, MT: Kessinger Publishing Company, 2010 (reprint).

Leaming, Barbara. *Marilyn Monroe*. New York: Three Rivers Press, 1998.

Little, William T. *The Tom Thomson Mystery*. Toronto: McGraw-Hill Ryerson, 1970.

Mady, Najla. *BOO!: Ghosts I Have(n't) Loved.* Toronto: Dundurn, 1993.

McCuaig, Ruth. *Our Pointe au Baril.* Self-published, 1989.

Mika, Helma and Nick. *Places in Ontario: Their Name Origins and History.* Belleville, ON: Mika Publishing, 1983.

Miller, Arthur and Serge Toubiana. *The Misfits: Story of a Shoot.* London: Phaidon, 2000.

Miller, Oro. *This Was London: The First Two Centuries.* Westport, ON: Butternet Press Inc., 1988.

Nicoll, Maurice. *Psychological Commentaries and the Teaching of Gurdjieff and Ouspensky.* London: Robinson & Watkins, 1974.

Petry, Bob. *Bala: An Early Settlement in Muskoka.* Lynx Images, 1998.

Spilsbury, John. *Cobourg: Early Days and Modern Times.* Cobourg, ON: The Cobourg Book Committee, 1981.

Stratford, J.P. *The Many Stages of Our Lives: Gravenhurst Opera House & Arts Centre, March 12, 1901–March 12, 2001.* Gravenhurst, ON: Gravenhurst Opera House, 2001.

Turcotte, Dorothy. *Burlington: The Growing Years.* Burlington, ON: The Burlington Historical Society, 1992.

Upton, Kyle. *Niagara's Ghosts at Fort George.* Self-published, 1999.

Victor, Adam. *The Marilyn Encyclopedia.* New York: Overlook Press, 1999.

Newspapers

Benne, Michael. "The Haunting of Halton." *Hamilton Spectator*, 1987.

Fragomeni, Carmela. "Halloween Busy for Canada's Top Ghost Hunter." *Hamilton Spectator*, October 31, 2001.

Goderich Signal, November 11, 1987.

Huron Expositor, February 20, 1880.

Parry Sound Star, Obituary Section, May 30, 1968.

Zuzyk, Ron. "Burlington Hotbed of Supernatural Phenomenon." *Burlington Post*, March, 2000.

Magazines

Cruickshank, Tom. "The Best of Bayfield." *Century Home*, June–July 1992.

Index

Other Books in This Series

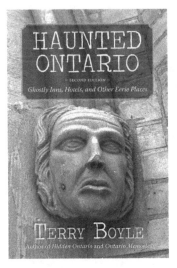

Haunted Ontario
Ghostly Inns, Hotels, and Other Eerie Places
Terry Boyle

Just when you thought it was safe to turn off the lights, ghost hunter Terry Boyle returns with a revised version of his bestselling *Haunted Ontario*. Join Terry as he conjures up a treasury of spectral delights that include apparitions at the former Swastika Hotel in Muskoka, the woman in the window at Inn at the Falls in Bracebridge, and poltergeists galore in Toronto's Royal Ontario Museum.

Venture — if you dare — on a ghost hunt to inns, hotels, and museums. Travel with your mind, and perhaps your body, too, to restaurants and private homes. Experience rattling doorknobs, slamming doors, faces in mirrors, and flickering lights. Read accounts from former skeptics and feel their nervous tension as they relate experiences of shadowy visitors, ghostly voices, and household objects that mysteriously disappear. Watch a television show when the set is unplugged and hear tales of vanishing sailors — boats and all.

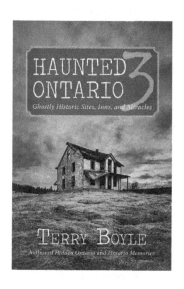

Haunted Ontario 3
Ghostly Historic Sites, Inns, and Miracles
Terry Boyle

Interested in discovering more about haunted Ontario? Join Terry Boyle as he explores the shadowlands beyond the grave. Revel in the outstanding evidence of spirit habitation in museums, historic homes, inns, jails, and graveyards. Witness the full apparition of the innkeeper's wife at Greystones Inn in Orangeville. Encounter the misty form of a civil war veteran in the graveyard of the old St. Thomas church. Experience the incredible slamming of doors at the Keefer Mansion in Thorold. Visit a whole village of spirits who share the buildings at Black Creek Pioneer Village. You can even spend the entire night in the Orillia Opera House with Terry and his friends.

Prepare to be scared out of your wits with the stories behind these and other hauntings. After providing you with a list of addresses, phone numbers, and websites for each location, Terry invites you and all other ghost enthusiasts along for the adventure. Feeling brave?

Of Related Interest

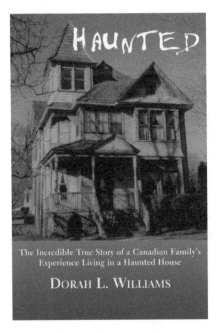

Haunted
The Incredible True Story of a Canadian Family's Experience Living in a Haunted House
Dorah L. Williams

It was an irrational decision. Despite having just moved into a beautiful new house, the Williams family gave in to an odd, overwhelming desire to purchase and move into a Victorian home they had come upon by chance. They were curious, of course, as to why the house had, in the past, had such a high vacancy rate — no one ever seemed to live in it for a long period of time. But that curiosity didn't last long, because shortly after moving in strange things began to happen. It became abundantly clear that the home's past owners had all had a reason for leaving: fear. The Williams' new home was haunted. At first, the family tried telling themselves there were logical explanations for the strange things they all were witnessing. But before long they came to accept the fact that they were sharing their home with ghosts.

Haunted is the Williams family's story from the point of view of the mother, Dorah. Through her chilling reminiscences, we witness the all-too-real goings-on in the house. And we join the family as they seek a way to bring an end to the paranormal events that were occurring with ever more frequency and intensity, and learn why the events began in the first place.

Meeting Place of the Dead
A True Haunting
Richard Palmisano

Come with us as we investigate a place that has so many spirits it is impossible to even hazard a count. A place that seems warm and inviting, but this is only an illusion — a ghostly trap to lure you in. On this journey we discover hidden secrets, violent ghosts who find enjoyment in attacking the living, and entities that disguise themselves as children. Discover why a paranormal investigation group with more than thirty years of experience had to shut down its investigations and walk away from an incredibly haunted property.

Paranormal investigator Richard Palmisano recounts the most sinister case he has ever faced. Join him in discovering the hidden secrets of malicious ghosts who lash out against the living, beings who mask themselves in false innocence, and a house so haunted Palmisano was forced to walk away forever.

Available at your favourite bookseller

VISIT US AT

Dundurn.com
@dundurnpress
Facebook.com/dundurnpress
Pinterest.com/dundurnpress